27 "E" Words That Will Change Your Life

Susan Chuey Williams Farah

AN OBSERVER AND FELLOW TRAVELER

BALBOA PRESS
A DIVISION OF HAY HOUSE

Balboa Press books may be ordered through booksellers or by contacting:

Balboa Press
A Division of Hay House
1663 Liberty Drive
Bloomington, IN 47403
www.balboapress.com
1-(877) 407-4847

Printed in the United States of America.

ISBN: 978-1-4525-7383-0 (sc)
ISBN: 978-1-4525-7384-7 (e)

Balboa Press rev. date: 7/1/2013

THIS BOOK IS DEDICATED TO ALL THOSE
WHO ARE STILL SEARCHING...

A special thanks to my husband, Tom, and my daughter, Stacey for all their love, support and encouragement.

Table of Contents

Prologue

"Let It Be"

-John Lennon

I believe we need to live our lives following our inner mantra that helps guide us through the maze we call our life. This silent guide who precariously tiptoes ever so lightly to try to avoid all the predicaments, pitfalls and potholes we get ourselves into. Sometimes, however, they get lost. You see, there's no "Garmin" so they are late to the party. And by this time we are already deep into the do-do and they are left trying to find a way to get us out, which isn't their job. It's not the job they were trained for so they aren't too good at it. In fact, they are pretty lousy at it. They are now our *fixer* not our guide. And as a fixer they were at the end of the line when someone was handing out all the fixing talents and they just got the leftovers and the fixer defects. So, we are left with a lousy fixer and no guide. And *we* are the ones who are lost.

So now we must do it scared. And if you've ever done it scared you are terrified. Terrified of the unknown and terrified of change. Why? How did it get to the point that we are so terrified of change? Change is all around us. Change happens every day to the earth, to everyone, to us. Why then are we so surprised when it happens? Why are we standing there with a look of panic on our face like a deer in the headlights? Why?

The only thing I have been able to figure out is that we have left our guard down. We actually didn't think it was going to happen to us. Ding, ding, ding! That's the bell for this round to be over during our boxing match called life. It can also be our wake up call – your wake up call.

Ding! Ding! Ding!

Wake up! Don't let life happen to you. You must happen to life. Let your inner mantra be "change is good", "change is good". Say it over and over again to yourself until it excites you. Say it until it ignites you. Only then can you get an aerial view of your life and begin to connect the dots, those crusty bread crumbs left by the architect. Those delectable crumbs that if we follow them become our passion.

Now let us begin our journey and concentrate on the things that make us the same and not the things that make us different. Too much time is wasted on looking at how we are different, meaning better, than someone else. Whose beliefs are better or "right"? Who has the right to be in charge? Who has the right to have more and who must have less? This has been our mistake. And unless we reverse this we truly are lost.

Who am I that you should want to take this journey

along side me? Well, I was born in 1953 in the bustling city of Youngstown, Ohio. And as a product of the "Baby Boomer" generation have observed and experienced all the social and environmental changes over the past sixty years that have not only produced great strides in knowledge and technology, but have also left great voids in the lives of people across the globe. It has been my personal journey as daughter, wife, mother, friend and citizen bridging the gap and ultimately steering my life raft to calmer waters that has brought me to you now.

For the last twenty seven years I have purposefully made it my priority as a healthcare professional, ordained minister, mentor and personal life coach to always *first* be a "nurturer and encourager". And as founder and Executive Director of Second Chances, a non-profit residential program for those with life-controlling problems, I had the privilege in helping individuals successfully realize their full personal potential. It is now my hope to inspire others to transform their lives and discover their ultimate purpose as nurturers and encouragers, too.

How is this going to work? Well, I have orchestrated this book of change into three sections. The first section is entitled "Act On It", which is exactly what it implies, words of action and ones you need to put action to if the change you want in your life is to be accomplished. The second section is entitled "Be It", or simply put, words that represent characteristics you must have if you are to change your life and truly live the life you want. The third section is entitled "Let It Be You", which I am not going to describe at this time. Hey, no tears, no moaning or groaning. You wouldn’t want to spoil the surprise, and be disappointed, would you? Well then, don’t read ahead and don’t read from the end of the book. Sit back and enjoy the ride. The joy is in the journey.

So my pioneer friend, are you ready to be transformed and inspired, to “Go where no man (or woman) has gone before”? That one was for all my “Trekkie” friends. Are you ready for a change? Are you ready to change? Good!

Our exploration begins…

ACT ON IT

Bradford Swift, a popular visionary non-fiction author, coined an idea that I like. When I heard it, it hit me hard, but in a good way. The idea is, be the CEO, Chief Executive Officer of your life. I like this idea because it makes me feel alive and full of possibilities. I also like this idea because it lets me know that I am second in charge, which means I am powerful, but I share this "road of life" with someone, I am not alone. Even though not all of us think alike and our beliefs may differ, one of those beliefs for most of us is that there is something bigger and greater than us, an architect. There are many names this "architect" has had and is now being called. I am not here to dispute any of them. I know my architect is God. You know who your architect is. And for the few of you who are reading this book and up to this point have not believed in the architect, I ask that you keep your mind open to the possibilities as you make the journey of reshaping your life back into the design it was meant to be, full of passion and highly inspired. And the first word is...

Embrace

I think it most appropriate that the first word we talk about, that will lead to your changed life, is one that is one without fear. For when you embrace someone or something you do it naturally and wholeheartedly, not timidly or with trepidation. *Embrace* – grab on, grab hold. Like a child grabbing for a toy they have wanted for a long time or a grown-up going for that preverbal brass ring. But even more than this, embrace implies that we just don't make a grab at it or make an attempt to do it. But that we encompass it with our arms outstretched, encircling it and pulling it towards us. So we can ingest it fully, embody it, savor it boldly and not miss a single drop of it!

So CEO, are you ready to learn some important facts about the word embrace? As a verb or action word, which for us is the way we are using it, definitions from the Bing Dictionary include: *"To make use of something, to welcome and take advantage of something eagerly or willingly."* Embrace the opportunity to change your life. "T*o adopt something, to take up or to take on something, especially a belief or way of life."* Embrace the new idea that change is good. "T*o comprise something, to include or support something as part of a whole."* A new way of life would be to embrace both love and forgiveness. "T*o surround something, to enclose, encompass, incorporate something."* His enthusiasm for life was so apparent it embraced his whole being.

Now that we have learned something about our first word what do we do next? You and I can do nothing like we often do when we learn an interesting or new fact. Just let it go into one ear and out the other. Let it go right through the red light or the stop sign of our brain and make it a fleeting memory of something we know we heard but can't remember what it was or why it was important to us. *Or* we can purposefully and intentionally make it stay there in our brain, in our consciousness and think. R*eally think* about it. Use the learning devise of application, thinking of ways we can incorporate it (aha - embrace) into our life. It will take work because you have become so accustomed to constantly taking in a steady stream of information, most of it useless, letting it flow in and out of your brain like a rushing stream that you have never given it a chance to leave an imprint of any kind behind.

It will take a change in the way you look at and process information to literally embrace these 27 words that will change your life. This is the reason why I chose *embrace* as our first word to tackle together. Mastering this "E" word is key to mastering the rest, and the tantalizing change you will experience!

Get ready, get prepared, let your body begin to tingle with anticipation and be impatient to turn this page and the next and the next. Are you tinkling? Are you chomping at the bit like a highly-tuned race horse at the starting gate anxiously waiting for the gate to open so you can win the race? If so, turn the page. If not, what are you waiting for? Hurry up and start tingling!

As the word *embrace* implies, what you do must be done

fully and with great passion and intention. Otherwise it is not embracing that you will be doing it will be something less, something lackluster, dull and boring. Limp and impotent to the requirements needed to change and revitalize your life.

So make a commitment from this moment on that whatever you do and whatever you believe you do it 100%. You give it 100% of your thought, time and energy. You give it your full attention like you would if you met your favorite movie star or sports figure or if $1,000,000.00 showed up on your doorstep, because this is just an important. In fact it is much more important. You must make it part of who you are and how you interact with people, how you make decisions and how you look at yourself and others.

You are probably saying to yourself "This is all well and good and easy for you to do but how do I do this? What are the mechanics"? Let me give you several steps to work on with some examples and then share a meaningful true story or two with you.

First, embrace each and every moment. It will never come again. In fact the twenty seconds it took me to write this sentence are gone, lost forever. Now if I hadn't typed this sentence the twenty seconds still would be gone and there would be nothing to show for them, nothing to mark their existence. There would just be a void and it would blend into the minute before and the minute after. But by embracing the moment and making the best use of its time, I have 100% *embraced* the moment. This is just one example of this step.

Someone else might have embraced those twenty seconds by reading a sentence out of an interesting book or Jane Doe down the street might have embraced her twenty seconds by sipping on homemade sweet tea while rocking in her rocking chair on her back porch. Yet another might have used their twenty seconds to feed a homeless person lunch at the local soup kitchen. The idea here is the embracing. Breathing in fully what you are doing while you are doing it and making it meaningful to you and others. And if it isn't meaningful for you or others, why the heck are you wasting your precious time, *time you will never have again,* doing it? So embrace your time, embrace your activities and embrace your thoughts. Ouch! That's a rough and tough one.

Thoughts. We waste a lot of time with negative thoughts, needless worrying and replaying minor infractions over and over in our heads. We think about things that will never happen. We think about things in the past. We think about things in the future. We think about things we did or didn't do and we think about things we wish we had said or didn't say. And what have we learned already? That's right. We can't get that time back so don't waste your time on needless thoughts and definitely don't embrace them and make them your reality. This brings us to number two, *embrace* people.

Literally embrace them, hug them and squeeze them. Tell them that you love them, respect them, miss them and want to be with them. Communicate through words and gestures just how much these people mean to you and do it today! Do not wait! We are not guaranteed tomorrow. Shoot, we are not even guaranteed the next five minutes. So stop procrastinating or waiting for the other person to make the first move. MOVE! Why is it we find it easier to pet a dog or a cat? Or a furry little bunny? And yet, we can't do the same with people? Are we afraid of rejection? Or are we afraid we won't look "cool"? I don't know but we need to quit it. Life really is too short. As you mature you realize too late all the people that you don't have anymore. All the people you wish you could just hug and squeeze and tell them that you love them.

Embrace the opportunity to help someone. Help a stranger. Believe me just about every moment of everyday there is someone within your reach who could use a hand in some way. It could be a word of encouragement (also an "E" word). It could be a smile or a "good job". It could be a sandwich or a warm blanket. Or it could be "I forgive you". Or, better still, "I am sorry, please *forgive me*". Think about it. Think about all the current relationships that could be improved with just a few minutes of your time. And then think of all the new relationships. You know, a word or a physical touch that reaches someone (or doesn't reach someone when it should have) affects that person. Whether you want to believe it or not, that is a relationship. Look for opportunities to embrace people.

Let me share a personal example with you. This example I am going to share with you happened more than once and now happens every time I do it. It has impacted my life greatly. I *pay attention*. That's it. "No, seriously, that really is it," I pay attention. I pay attention to me whether I am paying attention or not. Instead of just walking through life, through a situation or through a relationship; I really listen, see, taste and smell it. Time after time I found myself walking down the sidewalk, down the aisles at the supermarket, or browsing the racks in a small local shop totally oblivious to who and what was going on around me. I'd go through the check out line, paying for my groceries and never looking up at the cashier. Or maybe looking up, but not really seeing them and then answering their questions without thinking or remembering what was said.

One day I realized this about myself and I didn't like it. I didn't like it at all. The next day I did the opposite of what I normally did. I made eye contact with as many people as I could. I initiated conversations with as many people as I could (perfect strangers in fact). I became interested in people and really wanted to talk with them and find out about them. Help them in any way I could. And I smiled. Do you know what happened? I felt better. *I felt better.* My mood was uplifted, I felt like I had accomplished something. My tank was full and I felt like a person not a robot just going through the motions of the day. I've tried this experiment over and over again and it always comes out the same way every time. It works!

This next piece is a barrage of ideas for you: Embrace who you are and what you believe. Know what you want and what is important to you. Make lists. Make a gratitude list *and* a bucket list. When life hands you lemons learn how to make lemonade out of them. Make it fun. Make it a game. See how good you feel. Smile. Laugh. Whistle. Sing. Watch a bird. Look at trees, the sky and flowers. Take a class. Learn something new. Don't be satisfied. Strive to learn. Make your life mean something. You are "your life interesting". It's all on you to do. Someone else won't do it for you. Someone else won't make you happy. You have to make yourself happy, and fulfilled. Be the best you can be and help someone else be the best they can be too!

Now if that isn't enough ideas and steps to take for you – then read on - there are 26 more "E" words left to convince you! Remember, you need to understand the importance of "embrace". As we identify and talk about the next 26 words you must be able to embrace them and their concepts. It will be through this embracing of new ideas, the unfamiliar and the provocative that the change will come.

So come on, let's change! And our next word is...

Examine

What are the facts about examine? From Merriam-Webster: *"To study some thing, to inspect or study somebody or something in detail." "Investigate something or analyze something in order to understand or expose it." "To test, interrogate or inspect."* Let's take a look at the diagram below. This concept exposes a unique way of looking at the word *examine* and how it can be used to change your life. Take a chance, keep an open mind *and* embrace!

EXAMINE:

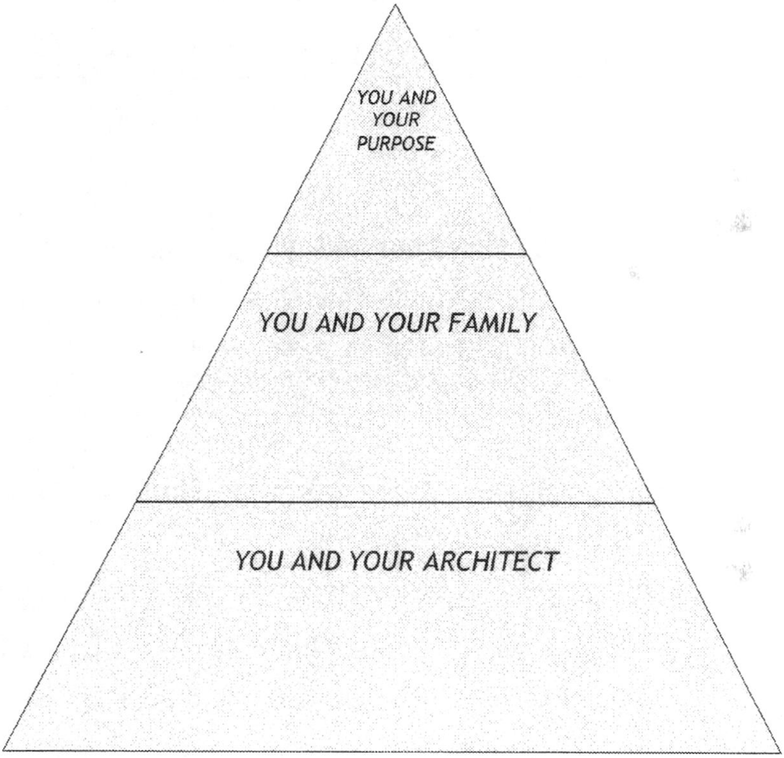

Self Examination Tool of the **“Life Essence Pyramid”**

Self Examination Tool of "The Life Essence Pyramid"

Pyramids are only stable if the bottom or foundation of the pyramid is broad and firm and grounded on something. So it is with life; my life, your life, our lives, all of us, all human beings. It needs to rest and to be built on something solid and the base needs to be constructed first before the rest of the pyramid, before the rest of our life. Think of it as all the raw materials you will need to build something.

This next exercise will help if you are sitting in a comfortable chair, in a quiet area with your eyes closed. Take a deep breath and then slowly exhale it. Next, in your mind's eye, envision all the necessary ingredients to successfully make something. It doesn't matter if you elect a cake to bake, a puzzle to put together or a toy airplane to build. The cake won't rise, the picture puzzle won't be complete and the toy airplane won't fly if you have left out even one ingredient.

So our Step #1 starts with the first tier of the pyramid "You and Your Architect" because this belief system and the emotions attached to it will affect everything you do in life (or don't do) and all your relationships (past, present and future). If we don't understand and master Step #1 we can't successfully make it to the top of the pyramid and achieve and embrace the fullness of our life's essence. A two-way communication and relationship with that which is greater than us, is *key* for quality relationships and quality of life that we all desire and aspire to attain.

This may initially sound a little radical but if you take the time to really think about it, it makes a lot of sense. It takes, belief, trust, faith, patience, and very good communication skills (both listening and speaking) to sustain any relationship for any period of time. If you are jealous, distrustful, envious, impatient, don't listen and then talk rudely or disrespectfully to people, that person will not stay in your life long - unless they are in a coma! You will have a revolving door of acquaintances because no one can become or stay a friend to someone who cannot be a friend. You will have a revolving door of jobs, people and activities in your life. That is unless you make pottery in a room by yourself just for yourself! So what can you do?

You can practice and perfect these skills and use your attributes along side your architect, who is the invisible source of energy that communicates to you through a sense of knowing and inspirations not billboards and a loud speaker. It forces all of us to pay attention to the details, look for the answers in the quiet time and spaces. Be patient, trusting and vulnerable enough to converse with someone we physically can't see or touch.

Relationships, jobs and hobbies can be had without taking Step #1 or even taking this pyramid seriously, many people do. And many people are unhappy, constantly searching and filling up their silent time with anything they can think of. Anything that they think will make them happy. Mid-life crises, addictions, over-indulgences, destructive behaviors and dependence on pills that "make us *feel* different or *be* different" run rampant in our lives and we can see them everyday in the tabloids and on the six o'clock news. Do you want to live like that?

So take this radical step as you examine yourself and take the plunge into putting Step #1 first and foremost in your life. For me, I choose to see my architect, God, everyday in everything, the good, bad and ugly. I thank him for the good, question and even complain about the bad and ugly and try to listen real hard to hear the explanations.

In this self-examination if you think your pyramid base is stable enough, then let's move on to Step #2: You and your family.

Now family can mean many things to many people. In our examination and for the purpose of getting a clear picture of your life essence, let's look at family in two categories. The first category we are going to examine is your "first family". These are the significant people in your life that have affected you either in a negative or positive way. They can be living or dead. They can be in your life now or not. They can be a birth parent you have never met or don't remember. This inner process of stepping outside yourself and looking externally to understand where you are in your internal essence is critical. It can also be scary and feel overwhelming.

Remember this is a process and there is no right and wrong, just progress. Let's talk about a few practical tips in looking at this "first family". I suggest you make a list of all the people from your past or your current life who illicit strong negative and strong positive feelings (there should be two lists). You can start with either list but doing the positive first would probably be the most beneficial.

Take one person at a time and really think about them and the effect they have had on your life. Write what comes to mind down on paper so it is tangible and feels very real to you. Read it out loud. This gives it importance to your being. Write about how they have changed your life or lead you in a positive way. What qualities do you have that you received or that were perfected through them? What interests or types of education or direction of vocation did they steer you towards? What qualities in them did you emulate? What did you admire in them? What hidden qualities did they encourage in you? Aren't these things what you want for your current family or "circle of influence"? So take the time to pass it on, pay it forward.

Now all of this should be pumping you up! You are going to need it because the next thing I am going to ask you to do is difficult. Take your second list, the one with the people who have influenced you negatively, and one by one think about them. It may be painful. Don't shoot the messenger here, but if it is painful, that actually is a good sign - because you have just indentified something that has been holding you back from being fully successful in your life. It may be holding you back from peace, joy, forgiveness, happiness and even love. It also may be holding you back from your all-important "secondary family".

Again examine what that person did or didn't do or say or didn't say that hurt you in some way. Then dissect how it affected your life negatively. Name It. Name the hurts. How did it feel? How does it feel now? How does it affect your relationships now, at home, at play or at work? Maybe you have never thought much about it. Maybe you just have "felt" mad or angry or ____. But think. Has this made you insecure, feel abandoned, needy, jealous, envious, controlling, distrustful or emotionally aloof? Have there been relationships or jobs you have lost due to those deep-seeded emotions raising their ugly heads wreaking havoc in your life? Have you fallen into addictions or abusive relationships? Have you been afraid to take chances or to believe and trust? Have you purposefully pushed people away rather then opening up and being vulnerable? Has the fear of being rejected, hurt, or made to feel stupid stopped you from doing something you really wanted to do? Or stopped you from having something you really wanted?

Examine...examine...examine...

This will take some time. Don't rush it. It won't happen overnight but taking each memory, remembering and working through it, then letting it go, will profoundly impact your life. My suggestion is that you forgive them and forgive yourself for holding on to it. Forgive your architect, in case you were blaming him for letting it happen. This doesn't let the "person" off the hook; it lets *you* off the hook, the hook of being tied to that person. That person has been weighing you down from your fantastic future. During this process you will also get insight into the negative actions and traits that you don't want in your life and that you don't want to inflict on your, yes you guessed it, "secondary family".

You know what's great about this part? When you finish it you have the choice to live life on its own terms; in your relationships, job and activities without being influenced subconsciously by the negative past. Have you ever wondered why you immediately dislike someone you just met? Or blow up at someone for no apparent reason? Maybe it's how they look, the tone of their voice or the way they move. Well, you don't have to do that anymore if you can master and tame your past. Don't continue to drag that baggage around with you anymore. It's too heavy. And you need empty suitcases so you have plenty of room to gather some wonderful memories and lots of exciting souvenirs.

Okay, once you have taken care of your "first family" let's move on to your "second". I think you probably have figured this one out already. It is identifying your family or close circle of people of influence now. *Those you have a responsibility to and are accountable to now.* They can encompass almost anyone you have let become important in your life. The list will be unique to each of us, and is a powerful portion of our relationships. Make sure this portion of your pyramid is as solid as your foundation. Work diligently on it. This middle portion of the pyramid develops from your foundational first level, is just as important, and the key to the development of the top of your pyramid, the third level and Step #3.

There are stories almost from the beginning of time about men and women who have missed their foundation, forgotten or neglected their families and put all their time and energy and passion into what they believe is their purpose. These are driven individuals who are out of balance with life, out of balance with their essence. Some of them, yes, have built empires but died lonely with no one at their funeral. And since you cannot (no matter what people think) "take it with you" what really did they have? Riches without love and peace, power without compassion and generosity, fear instead of respect. Creating a life with no essence, no essence to be emulated.

Consider the internationally-renowned news journalist spending his whole life searching out the truth in others and dying without finding the truth in himself. Working up until the day he died. Having no time to spend with his family and share together the great stories and wealth he had accumulated. And since, yes here it is again, you cannot take it with you, what part of his life would you label successful and fulfilled? We have an obligation to pass on our legacy to the ones who come after us, the next generation. Because of our age and experience, we know things and have first-hand knowledge they don't, but need, even if they think they don't. That is the beauty of maturity – you realize you know less than you thought you did. You must turn to the "elders of the tribe," keepers of the years of wisdom, whose wisdom can only come from years of turning their mistakes and obstacles into opportunities.

So, if you believe you are now ready we will proceed to the top of the pyramid, to the third level and Step #3. I call this the dessert because you can't live on dessert alone. It may taste great for awhile but if you dine only on it you will get sick and eventually parts of you, of your life, will die.

The first truth about Step #3 is that to be totally successful in it you must have a full grasp of and have mastered Steps #1 and #2. It's a progression principle and you can't skip steps. So logically your relationship with your architect and your relationships and responsibilities to your family are your first priority for your life's purpose. In religious teachings it is clear the time and energy spent between you and your architect, (your source or creator) and you and your family is most important. It must be. It must be quality time and energy, not just a few minutes here and there as an afterthought. It must be important to you. It must matter because you understand this is where your truth and the "you" of *who* you are come from, not from a job or a cause. So let's call Step #1 and #2 the common denominator of your life.

Understanding all of this, if you are ready to learn about #3, take out a pencil. You may want to write some of this down. "Remember in school when the instructor would teach something new and you were expected to learn it and then there would be a ____?" *"What is that thing called?" "A what?" "A test?" "A test - don't be afraid to shout it right out when you know it".* These lines are from the movie, "My Cousin Vinnie". Boy, Vinnie sure knew just how to make someone look smart and dumb all at the same time, didn't he?

Well, literally if you have mastered the first two steps you have been tested. Some general questions to think about might be: Are those relationships flourishing? How much quality time and energy am I spending maintaining and improving them? Where have I failed? How did it make me feel when I succeeded and when I failed? Because there will be days when you will fail. No one is perfect (good to know) and there will be times when you blow it! Get over it and get on with it. Make the next moment count. That's the secret. Don't let "you" beat yourself up and don't use it as an excuse to stop trying. No excuses!

Okay, let's move on to #3, "You and Your Purpose". I am going to give you a quick and easy example. Mother Teresa. I think we all know who she is. Mother Teresa was a nun but was that her purpose? She fed, ministered to and loved the poor of the poor, the undesirables and untouchables of India, was that her purpose? Was any of the above her purpose or was it what she did? Was it what she did as part of her vocation, her job? What do you think? Any of the above is admirable, and a case could be made for each of them being her purpose for being on this planet.

But I challenge you, what if her purpose was to inspire

others to examine their lives and search for their purpose? Or, what if her purpose was to shame governments, organizations and individuals into using their time, energy and resources to help those people? What if her purpose was to help one particular person or to inspire one particular person, and the thousands and hundred of thousands of people who were also affected, were just the extra that happened (the icing on the cake) while she was completing her purpose? One thing I do know she was not just here on this planet to win the Nobel Peace Prize, but she did.

What did you learn here? I hoped you learned the main principle behind Step #3: Your purpose is not necessarily what you do (even though there is some "doing" involved) but your purpose is more about "why" and "who" not just "do". Your purpose is usually all tied up with who you "are" and your essence, your life essence. And that is going to take a little while to sort out. We will be going in depth on the word essence a little later (yes you guessed, it starts with an "E"). There are so many other examples we can talk about here, but I want to share one from my own life with you.

To become a successful daughter, wife and mother takes an entire lifetime to accomplish. But once I personally understood the importance of it, I worked harder at it. As a nurse, mentor and counselor I have held many different positions all needing special and unique skills. Unknown to me at the time, those skills were also ones necessary to move me on towards my purpose. You see being a daughter, wife, mother, nurse, mentor or counselor isn't my purpose. I do know that. But

I had to master all the areas of my life revolving around my relationships before my purpose became clear to me. I know my purpose is to encourage others and empower them to be the best they can be. Not to be like someone else. But the best *they* can be. And *their* best will help them find *their* purpose and fulfill *their* life's essence.

I realized in some small ways I have been doing that since I was nine years old. I have also realized that without all the experiences, acquaintances and trials along the way - it wouldn't have been possible. Without them, even the bad ones, I would not be where I am today, writing this book in the hopes that it will encourage and empower you to be the best you can be and find your purpose and actualize your life's essence.

One last thing I wanted to leave you with before we move on is this - a "ponderance". What is a ponderance? Well, it's when you hear something that makes you go "hmmm" and you have to ponder on it, and it makes you think in a direction you haven't thought before. Kind of like something you might learn in a philosophy class. So here goes my "ponderance". What if a person's purpose appears to be something negative? Aha! Let me give you an example from a book by Dr. Wayne Dyer "Inspiration – Your Ultimate Calling". Dr. Dyer believes that his father, who was an alcoholic and abandoned his wife and three sons, had a purpose. His purpose was teaching his son forgiveness, which was critical in his ability to fulfill his purpose of inspiring others. So are we saying that it is possible to learn as much from the bad circumstances as we can from the good? If so, *we* can learn just as much from the negative that has happened to us in our life as from the positive. Ponder that one for awhile.

Do you feel like a CEO, Chief Executive Officer yet? Maybe just a small inkling of one, say a "C"? Okay, "C" let this rolling stone gather no moss! Let's move on to the next word which is...

Wait. Wait!

Just a little comic relief before we move on. I must tell you about some shows I have been watching on TV that has really expanded my mind. Okay, maybe that is an overstatement. Maybe it's more like they have been a truly eye-opening experience. These shows are someone's reality and are also good for a belly laugh. The shows are "Pawn Stars", "Storage Wars" and "Duck" something. I saw it for the first time last night so I don't remember the whole title but I laughed so hard I cried. You could literally build your philosophy of life on these three shows; if you were a golf ball, an abandoned box or a dusty old toy lying around in Aunt Janie's or Uncle Moe's attic.

On the surface the only thing these shows appear to be full of are; rednecks, tattoos, men with too many gold chains hanging around their necks and testosterone. But I have learned no matter how dumb something appears or how dumb the situation a person gets them self into is, the better the opportunity for me to remember to *THINK* before I act so I don't end up just like them. I believe that must be the philosophy the creators of these shows had in mind. So, if you don't want to end up a laughing-stock story on "Pawn Stars", "Storage Wars" or "Duck whatever" think before you speak, act or make that decision. Now, if you want to have a good laugh and later think how lucky you are not to be them, watch these shows. But first, a word of wisdom, don't let your shotgun totting uncle come with you when you go to the driving range. Those little white golf balls look too much like skeet and you might just find yourself stuck with a bagful of bullet-riddled ones. Look out! Fore!

That's it! "Duck Dynasty".

Okay, back to the important thing at hand, our third word:

Engage

Engage has numerous meanings as an action word, too. Here are a few from the Merriam-Webster Dictionary: *"To draw into, to involve or attract."* The speaker engaged his audience with his exciting tales. *"To take part or participate." "To enter into conflict with."* The enemies engaged into battle at the break of dawn.

Is it possible to live life without being engaged in it? Yes and no. You have to at least be partially engaged or else you wouldn't be alive. But you can go through life engaged on such a low level that it appears you are sleepwalking, or even somewhat semi-comatose. I know because I have done it myself. I was a wife and mother and went to work five days a week, talked to people and showed up at family holidays. I even smiled and laughed occasionally, but it was what I like to call "deadwood living". I was technically conscious, alive and breathing. My body was going through the motions on auto-pilot but there was no feeling or passion involved. I did things. I did my duty and fulfilled by job descriptions, but my heart and soul, my emotional being was somewhere else. For me, I was so internally confused and unhappy because I believed I had settled for less in my life. I was not where I wanted to be, or doing the things I wanted to do, so I shut off the part of me that could feel. And honestly, it took me nearly twenty years to reverse this and I still have some days when I feel I haven't "arrived" yet. So I know first hand, this "living without full life engagement" is possible. You can fool others. You can fool yourself. But you can't fool your architect. Hopefully one day you will be revealed.

But what does it truly mean to be fully engaged in your own life? What does it look like and feel like and how do I get it, you ask? These are all questions you should be asking yourself right about now and expecting me to give you the answers. Again, I am going to say a phrase that fits this situation "Pay Attention". If you don't pay attention life will wash over you and you will begin to be "deadwood".

Here are some hints: When you hear something, listen to what is really being said, don't automatically agree or brush it off. Practice questioning it, or using our definition three, have some conflict with it. Challenge it. All of a sudden you will "feel" more alive, your senses become more acute, and you will be interested in what you are questioning. So push the envelope!

Hint number two: Don't just do because you have to, do because you want to. Now you may say "Hey, I don't want to take out the garbage but I *have* to". True, but turn your *have* to into a *want* to, flip the switch, it's just like turning lemons into lemonade. Make a game of it if you have to. Do whatever works for you to take a duty, or an unattractive chore or obligation, and make it great! We are creative beings. We were made this way. Our brains can make us believe anything, so use that "creative brain matter," and create your way into a changed life. If you are having a little trouble doing this at first, try this:

Look at what's in your garbage bag and make up a story about it. Maybe it's the remnants of a trip across the United States or a trip to Italy (that's where I want to go). Make it about all those exciting cities you have been to and the fun you have had, the people you have met. And the kicker is you cannot go on another fun-filled journey until you throw away that bag of garbage, and get a clean, empty bag to start filling up with more unusual tidbits. If you dare, take it one step further. Pull out a book or go to the internet and start reading about these countries and cities you want to go to. Look at the pictures, get infused with the knowledge and let it stir up the passion in you. Then guess what? You are engaged in your life. You have just turned taking out the garbage into an event to be embraced (aha) in your life. And as a sidebar you may actually meet and talk to the person picking up your garbage and "thank" them. What a revolutionary thought!

This next one involves definition one, which as I said before is my favorite, engaging others, attract and hold the attention of others. Which is a natural need that us humans have because we want people to notice us, listen to us and pay attention to us, right? Then why are we so bad at engaging others? Do you think it might be because we are engaging for "our" benefit and not for the benefit of others? Hmmm....?

Aaahhh! Got us again! That's the problem. We are so worried about trying to engage with the other person to get them to listen to *us*, get them to agree with us, get them to like us, to validate us, us, us, us, that we miss the truth: IT'S NOT ALL ABOUT US!

What if we all took the attitude of making acquaintances, building new relationships and friendships, and doing things that involve others and made it for "them," for the other person? What would happen? What would happen if we got out of the "ourselves" and "it's all about me" syndrome and made it about the other person? See the situation from their point of view and through their eyes. Making it not about what they can do for *us* but about what we can do for *them*?

Again, revolutionary!

The bottom line is take every minute of every day of your life 100% and be a part of it. Don't let it live on without *you* because it will, if you let it. You have the power, don't give it away. Well now, we've done a little homework and now it is time to take what we have learned and put it together and do a "practice run". They say practice makes perfect. So Chief, let's get on the road to perfection.

So far we have talked about three words; embrace, examine and engage. What do they tell us? For me, they scream "Nothing happens in a vacuum!" Simply put, nothing happens by itself. Whether you choose to choose, or you choose not to choose, you still have made a choice. And depending on what you have chosen, will become your life. So choose wisely. Not choosing at all is still a choice. I would much rather make the choice myself then to let someone else choose for me. Right or wrong, good or bad, blessings or consequences, we reap what we sow and we gather what we have planted. You can't expect to get corn if you have planted soybeans. So if you don't want to end up with soybeans, or something you don't want, you better get busy doing and planting so you get the results and the life *you want*! If you are afraid to choose and just let life happen, or let someone else choose for you, guess what? You can't blame *them* if it doesn't turn out the way you wanted it to. You chose to do nothing, so you let it happen. So, if it is fear that is driving you, the fear to choose, you probably will end up with what you don't want anyway so you might as well choose something. Choose for yourself. Take action. Be the one in the driver's seat; be the CEO. Be the CEO of your life!

You may say it's not fear that is holding me back, its money, time, my age, where I live, my family, my lack of education, my physical handicap and the list goes on and on. Boulderdash! Start today and make it the first day of the rest of your life!

Embrace each day, and moment, and opportunity fully. Examine your life and truly see the hierarchy of your life priorities and pay attention. Be engaged in your own life and engage the lives of others. Nothing changes until something changes. And your life won't change until *you* start to make a change – let that day be today! Be the catalyst that starts the first domino to fall and stand back, and see what happens.

There's someone out there who is saying "I'm still clueless, I need an example". Okay, for the clueless, let's see if this helps:

It's a new day. I walk out my door embracing the notion that I am here on this planet to encourage others and inspire them in such a way that enables and empowers them to reach their full potential and inspire others. Because I embrace that idea about myself, I walk out the door with my eyes wide open, my antennas (ears) tuned in; and my "pay attention" barometer on 100%. I intentionally look for people to talk to, situations to be involved in, opportunities to help someone, and opportunities to learn something new. I am ready to tell my story and ready to listen to someone else's story. When I encounter someone who needs help in some way I examine my past experiences, my finances and my motives, and put myself into their life (engaging) by assisting however I can. By doing this, I am now engaged in a relationship with this person. It may only last a few moments, or it may last a few years. The point is; I have pulled that person into my world. This is my idea of inspiration, empowerment and potential. See?

Let's move on to word number four and see how it fits into our equation:

Envision

Did you know that the first time someone used the word "envision" was in 1855? What do you think they envisioned? Who do you think said it for the first time? Don't you know, this is an excellent (again the "E" word) bit of trivia for you to share at your next party. The Merriam-Webster Dictionary defines envision: *"To picture to oneself."* She envisioned a new life for herself.

See it, feel it, it is yours!

I believe that whatever we want to do, or have, or to be, must first start with a thought. Then we take that thought to the next level and **embrace**, **examine** and **engage** it. In other words, we first make it happen in our heads before we can make it happen in our lives. To do that it must become absolutely real and attainable in our *mind*. Then, it must go a step further. It must become absolutely real and attainable in our *heart*. We must believe it is possible. And ultimately we must believe it is attainable *for us*.

Aha! Did you see I added the "for us"? Snuck that one in on you didn't I? We waste our time making a list of all the reasons why we "can't". We spend too much time believing that what we want others already have. Subsequently, we become jealous or envious (another great "E" word to think about) and miserable. So much time is wasted looking at others and what they have (possessions), or are doing that we want to do (vacations, jobs, relationships), that we miss the point: They have already envisioned it and attained it for themselves while we were whining and "stuck on stupid". "Stuck on stupid", I really like that phrase.

I wonder where that one came from and who coined it. Were they stuck in the mud and said "Boy, is this stupid"? Or was it more like "Stupid is as stupid does", thank you Forrest Gump, from the movie, Forrest Gump. Either way, there's a stuck stupid that needs unstuck. So let's take a closer look at it.

AA names it "stinking thinking" and your teachers and parents used to call it "You better change your attitude or else." Or the classic, "You better take this in before I take you out!" It's negative, woe-is-me thoughts and thinking of all the reasons why it can't or won't happen. Making a list in your head of all the reasons why for *you* it will never happen. So, here's the challenge. Every time a negative thought pops into your head you have to take hold of it, take it captive. Kidnap it! You must take control of your thoughts otherwise you will continue to think negatively which causes you to act contrary to the "thing" you want. Everything must be in alignment, thoughts + words + actions = the end results you want. What does this mean for you? It means for you to be successful you must do two things:

Do you mean the "first thing or the second thing"? That

one I got from the movie "Analyze This". You just gotta love Robert DeNiro and Billy Crystal in "dat" one. Anyway, you must envision what you want and stop envisioning what you don't want. It's a two-way street or for our purposes, it's a two-way thought process. You can't envision yourself as a high-school English teacher and then constantly tell yourself all the reasons why you can't become one: "I don't have the money. I'm not smart enough. No one in my family has ever gone to college. What will my "hanging out at the corner" friends say? It will take too long. No one will hire me." The list goes on and on. If you do this, the "second thing" will counteract the "first thing" – the *envisioning*. It will be null and void, and neutralized. Again, all thoughts, words and actions must be in alignment. All race cars must be going around the racetrack in the same direction or there's going to be a bad accident, a 30-car pile-up and no one crosses the finish line. No one wins!

You have to see yourself and feel yourself in that end-result, what you want. You must see yourself at the college of your choice. See your self studying and passing those tests. See yourself walking down the aisle and accepting *your* diploma from the Dean of the English Department. You must feel the excitement and the butterflies in your stomach as your fingers wrap tightly around that piece of sheep-skin. See the tears of joy in your family's eyes. Feel the pride welling up inside of you at your accomplishment. See yourself standing in front of the classroom teaching those kids. Then put what you have seen and felt into words. Let's call them - words of encouragement (another great "E" word). Words of optimism, words of a dream come true, and words of fruition. Because as you see it, and feel it, then match up your words with what you are seeing and feeling you are literally "real"ing it into existence. You have already accomplished it, it is already done. So now all you have to do is to live it out. *You are what you believe.* You have what you *believe* you deserve. You have believed it for yourself. You have envisioned it. You have made it real and put it into existence as a living, breathing reality.

Now, all that is left is just following up, following the map, and retracing our steps. It's simple. Simple, I didn't say easy. That would be silly. It is still going to take doing all those things, you putting hands and feet to them and overcoming the obstacles (opportunities) that will come up along your journey to the finish line. But you *can* handle them. You have already seen the finish line; you can come up with a solution, a plan and execute it (put it into action, not kill it). Hey, and remember to include your architect. Architects who build houses always have the floor plans, full of the details needed to build that perfect home. So why wouldn't your architect already have the perfect floor plans for you? The one you need to navigate and steer your life in the right direction.

Is this beginning to fall into place for you?

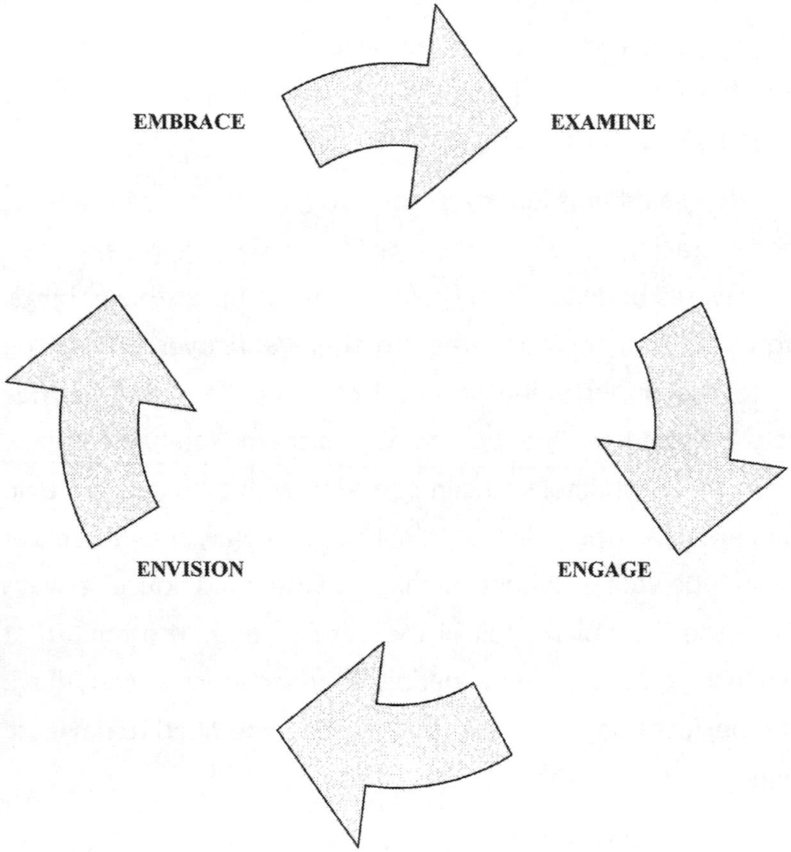
EMBRACE
EXAMINE
ENGAGE
ENVISION

If you haven’t realized it yet, we have been building. Building that purpose-filled life you want. The one you were meant to live out. Teamed up with your architect, who has already laid out the plan, you are building the life you were meant to live. A life built with solid materials and a firm foundation. Sounds good, doesn’t it?

Let me talk a few more minutes about the “second thing”. I think you probably understand the “you need to see yourself doing, feeling and speaking what you want” part. But getting those negative forces that try to sabotage your goal under control may need a little tweaking. First, it isn’t just what pops into your own head that puts you down, or what you try to talk yourself out of that’s the problem. It is everything else and everyone else who is doing it that you are going to have to learn to deal with. This sometimes can be harder than dealing with your self. So let’s talk examples:

First, some examples of what your responsibilities are. You have to study to pass those tests. And if you are having trouble, it is *your* responsibility to find a tutor so you can pass those tests. This is not magic. There is no “poof” and you’re a teacher. You have to do all the things required to become one. But you CAN do it! Remember, you have already seen yourself as one.

I have a paperweight on my desk that reads: “Act as if it were impossible to fail”. I believe that one-hundred percent! I believe it is impossible to fail. I believe it is impossible for you to fail. You may not succeed at everything you attempt but that does not mean you have failed. It means you are on the road to success. It means you have learned something that is now invaluable to you, and to your success. *All* things are possible. Collaborate with your architect. Go back to the drawing board and together you *can* make it happen.

At this point, I want to be perfectly clear. I am not talking about conjuring up a BMW, or Mercedes or a house in the Hamptons. This book is about taking your life, making the most of it, and being the most you can be. Knowing your life purpose and passion, making the changes you need to, and then turning it into the fulfillment of your life, the essence of who you are. I just wanted to make myself clear. No hocus-pocus. No, "Let's get some bling-bling."

Look inside. Look inside yourself. What are the intrinsic factors that make you "you" and have reaped the successes and the "un"successes in your life so far? The positives you need to build on. The negatives you need to throw out. Remember, your life is not just one big long day. It is broken up into segments, 24 of them to be exact. So make each one a new beginning. "Great!" If you mess up today you'll have a clean slate tomorrow. True, but also remember, if you do something incredibly wonderful today, by tomorrow that wonderful is yesterday, and the slate is clean again. Clean to work on replicating that success. You can't bask in yesterdays' sun because today's another day. In the same way, don't beat yourself up about a mistake from yesterday, you can't go back, but you can go ahead and replace the wrong with a right. And make it right, make it a success.

Don't tell yourself you can't or you will never be. Since we are what we believe we are, the better self-talk would be: "I am becoming a teacher. I am one day closer to graduating and becoming a teacher. When I become a teacher I will _____." If you have people in your life who tell you that you can't – neutralize them. Maybe not with a "set phasers to stun," *neutralizer* gun like they used in Star Trek, but you do have the power to wipe them out. You can choose to not listen to them, and replace the negatives they are saying with positive self-talk in your head. You can tell them it is unacceptable what they are saying about you and they must stop. Or you can remove them from your life or remove yourself from their life. Different approaches are needed depending on the situation. These are just a few examples.

You may not have the resources initially to get to the education you need. I hope you noticed I said initially, because this is where we as "creations" as creative human beings, comes in. There literally is no problem without a solution. No obstacle without an opportunity waiting to solve the problem. And if I can be ironical here, when we are talking about your life's purpose, your true passion and your realized fulfillment, it's not supposed to be easy. Then you would have no need for your architect. You could just zip-zap, do it. Then how could you truly be inspirational to someone else who is struggling? Oh no, maybe there's more to this than meets the eye. We'll discuss that one a little later. But seriously, if it is too easy it may not be your true passion. It may be just what you are feeling or what you are now or what you want now until you realize there's something more.

Think about this: Once there was a little boy and his father and mother were both lawyers. He grew up in a household that had the money, the knowledge and the connections to get him into law school. His mother and father expected him to be a lawyer. He didn't really think much about it because it was assumed by everyone he would be one and he figured it would be easy. And it was for him. He became a lawyer and by the age of 50 had been married three times, had an ulcer and high blood pressure, four children and a grandchild he hardly ever saw - and he hated his life. One day he woke up and said, "What the hell happened to my life?" He had a house, and several fancy cars, a large bank account and portfolio, but he didn't have joy, passion or satisfaction in his life.

He dreamed he was 16, with a small group of his friends playing their guitars. He loved music and he had been good at it. In fact, his music teacher in high school had encouraged him to pursue his music further, but he had been afraid. He had been afraid to tell his parents, afraid of failing and afraid of not being important in his parent's eyes – afraid. So he said nothing, nothing at all. Eventually he stopped playing and never picked up his guitar again. He would imagine he was a rock star, or a country guitarist writing his own songs and playing them in small clubs and bars. Sometimes after hearing a song on the radio from his past, anger would well up inside him for no reason. The anger would be so raw that he would take out his frustration on the next person he saw.

Now, how do you think this story turns out?

What could he do to change his life? Should he?

A lot to think about, isn't it?

What have you designed for your life so far? How it is working out for you? Did you think it up or let it happen to you? Why are you reading this book?

Let me share something personal with you. About thirteen months ago I knew I had to write a book. Now, I had never written one before, really didn't know how to go about it, didn't have an editor or publisher, but I knew that I knew I had to do it. So I just sat down in front of the computer and starting typing. I typed like I thought. And the more I typed the more I thought, and the more I thought the more I typed. It was just me putting my thoughts down on paper. But all of a sudden it was more than me just emptying the stuff out of my head. It was more because it was my passion, I loved it. It's what made the rest of my day and all the other stuff I had to do; chores, job, paying bills and dealing with people, bearable. I was having fun. I was creating something. I've learned along the way we are always creating. Whatever you have made of this day, you have created it for yourself. But this was more than that. I felt alive and powerful in a way, more like empowered, by doing it. I was empowered to do more.

And if I can even be more transparent, not only did I know that I was supposed to write that book but at least nine in all. In fact, I had the titles of nine books in my head. I wrote them down. Then I typed them up and titled my list: "Books I Have

Been Inspired to Write". Each of them I knew something about – a hint of what each one would be – but not everything. The rest I knew would be revealed to me when it was time. Time... friend or foe? For me, at this time, it's my friend. If you are reading this book (my fourth) then you are part of the truth of "It can be done". Because I know if I can do it, you can do it too. You can embrace your passion and what you have envisioned for your life. What you have envisioned for yourself!

Read on...

What makes *you* feel totally alive? What makes you want to jump out of bed and start running before your feet hit the ground? That's passion. That's *f*rom somewhere down deep, deep inside, where your spirit and soul reside. So what have you envisioned for yourself, for your family and what kind of world have you envisioned you want to live in? If you think that one person can't change the world – you are wrong. It just takes one. It just takes one voice. Be that voice.

Next...

Are you panting with anticipation to know what our next word will be? Are your hands trembling so hard that you can barely turn the page? I hope so. It's important to be excited about a word that can change your life. This word that holds so much importance we will be devoting several pages just to talking about it. What could this all-important word be?

Exhale

Exhale?

Really, that's the important word?

Yes, because I realize that every time I exhale I learn something new.

So much of our lives are spent being intense and busy, trying to be as productive as we can be, because we believe we must or we will miss something important. And we are right, but the something we will miss is exhaling. Take in a big deep breath, hold it a second then let it all out, *all* the way, until your lungs are empty and the next breath you take is 100% fresh.

Let me tell you what I learned today as I exhaled. I have been using a word incorrectly. It is one that I have used a lot. So you can imagine my surprise when I realized I have been making this mistake for years. Now there are times when it isn't so important to use every word correctly, or know the exact meanings of words, but when you are trying to communicate something you feel is important to someone else, well, it is. Unless you are trying be funny and be wrong on purpose. But in my case, I wasn't trying to be wrong or funny. I was just wrong. So here is my learning curve for the day.

I have been using the word analogy for all my comparisons. So what to my wondering eyes and befuddled brain should appear this morning but simile. Now simile is like smile with an extra "i" (Get it? Simile is like smile with an extra "i" – my case in point). It's a simile not an analogy.

If learning that wasn't bad enough, metaphor and idiom came along with simile for the ride. And to make matters even worse I realized I have used idioms just as much as similes and called them all analogies. Now, is this earth-shattering or life-changing? No, not really. But as I speak to you through my writing, it is important that I use the right words. I would have continued to miss the importance of this if I hadn't taken the time to exhale today, to *make* the time to exhale today. This was my "exhale gift" for today and I would have missed it.

So let me share what I learned and then let's take a trip and exhale.

Analogy - kitten is to puppy like cat is to dog

Metaphor – her hair was silk

Simile – her hair was *like* silk

Idiom – burn the candle at both ends (to exhaust yourself by doing too much - if both ends of a candle were lit it would burn out faster). *And so would you!*

Now exhale...

Merriam-Webster says that exhale is: *"To breathe out or to emit breath."* (no example needed). *"To rise or be given off or to give forth."* I like this second definition a lot. But it is in the combination of both of these definitions that will give meaning and power to what we have been talking about.

Common sense tells us that we cannot be at our best, be 100% effective, be wonderfully creative and a "joy" to be around, if we are tired and cranky, over-worked, stressed and physically, mentally, emotionally or spiritually depleted. If this describes you then you are pretty much useless until you get refreshed, rejuvenated and are running on a full tank of gas. So take a break, take a day off or a week off, laugh, walk on the beach, paint a picture, go to the park and throw a Frisbee with your dog. Have fun! Try to remember what "fun" was for you when you were a kid, and do it! Be absurd. Wear a funny hat or paint a handlebar mustache on your face and pretend you are an Italian barber or an organ grinder. Sing out loud while you are driving your car and then watch the reactions of the people watching you. Don't take yourself so seriously! Enjoy, take it easy and relax. Take a vacation from your life for a few hours or a few days.

Escape. Plan a prison break and break *yourself* out of jail. Pay attention to the big red flashing exit sign, follow the directions, and exit! Turn off the ADD and ADHD of your mind and quit thinking! Let go of the schemes. Quit trying to figure things out or come up with the perfect plan. Let it go. Watch it go bye-bye and fly away. Wave to it and wish it a fond farewell. Once your mind is clear and your body refreshed, you will be amazed what ideas and unique solutions your mind will come up with to those serious questions or problems that have been weighing you down. Suddenly, you will find yourself feeling smarter than you thought you were, and solving the unsolvable, conquering the unconquerable, and doing the "Don Quixote" thing and not only "dream the impossible dream" but *do* the impossible.

Exhale...

I find that I have the best ideas and those "aha" moments when I am in the bathroom or driving in the car. Really, almost every smart idea I have come up with came during an encounter with my bathroom or behind a steering wheel. I suppose the "car thing" happens because I am so focused on the road, the other cars, and not getting picked up by the police; that I allow my thoughts to wander into a different compartment of my brain where the "brighter bulbs" are hiding and then *Eureka*! The light bulb goes off and starts to shine at a bright 100 watts and not the dim 40 it has been limping along at.

But the bathroom one I am a little confused about. Is it to make me feel silly or bring me down a peg or two? Maybe it's to let me know that with a toothbrush in my mouth and white foamy toothpaste dribbling and drooling down my face, my architect can bring out a more exhilarating and luminous idea that is absolutely perfect. While on my own I have struggled in my studious and professional demeanor for days and weeks and have come up empty. The joke is on me, or literally the toothpaste is on me. So again, be the first to laugh at your self. Enjoy the journey, enjoy the ride. It's the ride of a lifetime. Don't waste it!

The other importance to exhaling and exiting is to get rid of your worries. They just make you look old and give you wrinkles, and frown and worry lines. Remember you can't control much of anything anyway. You can't control people, the weather, the economy, politics or people fighting about religion, or if a dog or a cat is a better pet. Personally I vote for dogs. They love you even if you forget to feed them and no fur balls. Heck, most times you can't even control yourself, so stop trying to control everything else and worrying about if you can or can't. Shut it off. Pull the plug. Turn off the light switch and pretend no one is home.

I dare you to walk through Walmart or better yet, your office building and sing "We're Off to See the Wizard" at the top of your lungs while skipping down the aisles. Or, this is a really good one, get on an elevator with one or two people you don't know and then start holding a conversation with yourself out loud; begin talking to yourself and then answering yourself back in a totally different voice. Climax the situation by having an argument with yourself. Get really irate with yourself and then get off the elevator on the next floor and walk away. Ha, ha, ha. Get it?! Ha, ha, ha.

Take time for yourself and do something that feeds your soul and lifts your spirit. Exhale. Let that big breath out and get in touch with that "child" inside you. We all have one you know. That "child-like" little elf inside us that every so often peek their little pointed head out and makes us look silly, or gets us into trouble. But more importantly, is the "playful" part of us. Get in touch with that elf-child and spend sometime getting to know them. Your elf may just hold the key you have been looking for, that special key that will unlock the secrets of your universe. You never know!

Have some fun...exhale.

Are you ready for some digging? You better be. Because our next word is:

Excavate

Excavate is a very close cousin to exterminate, eradicate, eliminate, eject, end and "enough is enough" – kinda like a "kissing cousin." So let's get busy. Pull out your pick and, your hard hat, and your work boots - it's gonna be bulldozing day.

Excavate implies hard work. It implies taking time and effort, and that is just what is needed now to realize a major change in your life. There are several definitions, but the ones I like best are from the Bing Dictionary: "To *uncover something with difficulty; to discover something valuable by effort;* to dig for artifacts." And finally, "To *dig in a place carefully and methodically, taking notes about procedures, conditions and finds with a view to uncovering objects of archaeological interest.*" Do you think there is something about your past that has archaeological value? Is there some undiscovered item of your past that once unearthed and removed out of your life will change you, free you?

How about excavating the remains of a temple? How about excavating the remains of *your temple*? That's right, your body, your soul, your spirit, is a temple. You were made to hold value and to be valued, and to share that value with others. Hurt and anger, resentments, unforgiveness and disappointments have eroded away at the beauty and the perfection of your temple, like termites. It's now time to end it! Stop it from happening and exterminate those "termites" which have been eating away at your foundation and your heart.

First, we must eject from our lives the lists of wrongs people have done to us and we have been holding on to. It's only hurting you *not them*. Is this radical thinking for you? Do you really think that by keeping alive everything everyone has done wrong to you that it was making *them* miserable? Really? Hey, they have already forgotten about it, moved on and probably are having a great life, while you suffer and say "woe is me, my life is ruined" about what they did.

"G-e-e-e-t over it!"

You are the one who is still hurting. You are the one being held back from a full and free life, not them. Let *yourself* off the hook and let go. But what if you think what they did is so terrible that they should be punished? That maybe true, but *you* holding on to it and continuing to let it ruin your life isn't punishing them, it's punishing *you*. "Yes, but if they see how miserable I am they will feel guilty and beg my forgiveness." You got to be kidding me. Are you serious? Are you really holding out for that to happen? Do you actually think it will? I would say in most cases hell would have to freeze over first. If they were going to beg your forgiveness they would have done it already. Making yourself a "tragedy" is what is *truly tragic*!

Do you think I am being hard on you? I am actually being loving and kind to you. I am trying to help you free yourself. No one else can but you. You have allowed someone else to put you and keep you in a cage for months, years, maybe tens of years. You have missed out on freedom and enjoyment of life because you want justice. You can't get it. You can't do a "revenge" on them, because then you are just as wrong as they are. And if we believe in the "We reap what we sow" principle (and I highly do) then let them get "theirs" another way and you get on with your life. Don't worry how they are going to get it, or when, or by who. Enough's enough! Hopefully, if the wrong done was something illegal, you were able to come forth. If not, that's okay. Again move on. This is about you and your life. This is about living your life to its highest fulfilled purpose. You can't do that with cement blocks tied to your legs – you're gonna drown!

So what are the steps to make this happen? The practical thing to do is make a list of all the people who you have negative feelings about, who you believe have harmed you. Then one by one think about that person and what they have done, write it all down on paper along with all the emotions it brings to the surface. Like a well or a natural spring when a torrid rain comes along. Let your feelings well up inside and overflow onto the paper like rushing waters. Then go somewhere quiet and safe and read it out loud pretending that person is there in front of you. Get it out, yell, cry, scream, yell obscenities at them if you have to, but get it *all* out for good. Then let it go. Say out loud, "I choose to forgive you and I choose to forgive myself for holding on to this." "It is over". Then do two more things. Take that paper and rip it up in tiny pieces or burn it, or bury it. Destroy it. This is a very important step because it is action and action is a powerful release and it finalizes it for you.

This next thing is really optional but I encourage you to do it. Close your eyes and envision that person is standing there with you in the room. Make it as real as you can, really concentrate. Can you see them? Can you feel them close by? Then close the door on them and walk away. It's okay to slam it if you need to, but nonviolence is always best. You have just released yourself from the past and now, or very soon you will know it. You will be different. You will feel different and see things differently. You have just annihilated the past, neutralized it. You have rewritten your present *and* secured your future. Woo-hah!

Congratulate yourself. Pat yourself on the back. You deserve it! Take yourself out to lunch and celebrate. Buy yourself a new pair of shoes or treat yourself to a night on the town. Call the florist, order flowers to be delivered to yourself in three weeks, have the card signed "From your secret admirer," then forget you did it. Three weeks later out of the blue flowers will be delivered to you and everyone will be guessing who they are from. Whatever you do *"do not tell anyone you sent them"*. Keep them guessing, you'll have a blast!

Now do this procedure with every one of those people on your list. One at a time and take your time. Remember the definition of excavate, dig carefully and methodically, take effort. The more effort you put into it, the freer you will be. And it's about time, isn't it?

It's *your* time.

There is one additional thing you can do. We used this when we had our faith-based center and were working with women with shattered lives. We would have them close their eyes and envision the person standing next to them in a room with a long hallway. At the end of that hallway was God or Jesus (you can substitute your architect here) with his arms outstretched. We would then ask them to take the hand of that person and walk them slowly down that hallway and put that person in the outstretched arms of their architect. They then would be asked to turn, walk back down that hallway, open the door at the end, walk through it, and close the door behind them – never looking back.

This is an incredibly powerful exercise. Whatever your beliefs are, whatever name your architect has, the eternal force and omnipresent energy is reality, no matter how you slice it.

Let me share a story of what happens when someone chooses *not* to let go, not to forgive. We had a student in our program, (let's call her Chloe), she was in her late 20's and a mother of two. The biological fathers of her children were not in the picture. Her children were being raised by their grandmother due to Chloe's drug and alcohol addiction. Our program was a year long, 24/7 residential life-changing "boot-camp". After Chloe was there a few months, her story emerged. At 13 she had been raped by a neighbor. He had never been brought to justice. The family more or less swept it under the rug. They tried to get her to forget it and "be okay". She wasn't. As often happens, she turned to promiscuity, drugs and alcohol. Chloe got pregnant at a young age and ten years later found herself an alcoholic, drug addicted mother of two, living with any man who would pay attention to her. Even if that attention was to beat on her.

Once in the program she made very good progress, and after eleven months we thought she might make it. But then a very sad thing happened. She had one last hurdle to climb. She had to forgive the man who had raped her. She had to let it go. This was her Achilles' heel and the core issue to her addictions and destructive behaviors. The inability to forgive and let go had control over her. She refused to do it. She logically understood that this was the only way she would be free, but she couldn't let go of her belief that if she forgave him she was "letting him off the hook". We couldn't get her to understand that *he* wasn't on the hook, *she was*. He had gone on with his life and was having a good one. He hadn't thought about her and what he had done in years. But she couldn't let it go. She left the program in the eleventh month only weeks from graduating. We didn't hear from her again. Her sister kept in touch with us for a while. She let us know Chloe was back out drinking and drugging, getting arrested and sleeping with man after man. She had permanently lost her children.

It's a sad story, isn't it? Do you see a little of yourself in Chloe? Not being able to forgive someone, or not able to let go of an insult or bad relationship? Don't let your pride get in the way. Forgive others and forgive yourself. This brings up another point: Maybe *you* are one that needs forgiveness from yourself and others. What about that? If this is the case, you need to do a list on yourself. Go through the same process as you did previously with the lists you have done. If you have hurt someone else, you need to try to make it right. *If* - and this is a big if, *if* by doing so you don't *hurt them more or hurt them again*. In that situation you need to think of the other person's feelings first. You can't make it worse for someone else just to make yourself feel better. That would be the epitome of selfishness!

Now that you have faced your past, it is time for the next step: Know yourself without delusions. Ouch! Sounds like more digging. "And now we are digging into me" you are saying to yourself. Yes! It's time to look deep inside and pluck out the obstacles standing in your way. Those things that have for years stood in the way of you obtaining success, of reaching your goal and soaring high as you become all you can be! It's time to be honest with yourself. No one is watching. No one can hear you. Say it out loud and once it's brought to light it isn't so scary anymore. It's not lurking waiting to pounce at any minute. It has been brought out into the daylight and in the sunlight it looks smaller, shrunken, and has lost its power. Your job now is to take away all of its importance, so this counter force cannot continue to steal your passion and purpose.

Your obstacles can be many things; from alcohol and drugs, to overeating and unhealthy lifestyles, to fears and procrastination. You can have one or you can have ten. Since we are all unique individuals our combination of counter forces like our DNA, and our fingerprints, are exclusive to us, distinctive. They are not something to be afraid of, or ashamed of, but if you choose to let it be, then it too becomes a counter force in your life. Blocking you from the fulfilled life you want. So *you* be the one to blow the whistle on yourself and excavate and eradicate these "nasty road blocks" from your life.

I wish I could tell you that just by identifying these road blocks you are done and they will go away. But that wouldn't be honest of me. Each one of these things you probably have had attached to you for quite awhile, so it is going to take some effort and expertise (another great "E" word), to help rid yourself of them. But rid yourself of them you must, if you want to attain and *maintain* your life essence and the health of your soul and spirit.

You may need to get professional treatment, an accountability partner, or life coach. You may need to look at the "triggers," your weak areas that put you in that downward spiral. Sometimes changing living situations or jobs or ending relationships needs to be considered. It may even be necessary to distance yourself from certain people or certain "people personalities". And you may have to intentionally and purposefully do things every day of your life to succeed, and not fall back into the traps, and the muck and mire. But it will be worth it.

This may sound, feel, or seem overwhelming to you at this very minute. Stop. Breathe. You can do this. Nothing is impossible, and there is no one who "can't". It is just a matter of doing what you can do today and realizing tomorrow is also a day, another day. And tomorrow you can do some more. Life truly is a process. "Run the race" always with the finish line in mind, and equipped with the knowledge that you can't cross the finish line without running the race first. So run! Run your race.

A few suggestions, a few tools that may help get you started and assist you along the way. They come in the way of a number of incredible books: "Boundaries" by Cloud and Townsend, "Search for Significance" by Robert McGee, "The Anger Workbook" by L. Carter, "The Five Love Languages" by Chapman, "The Mom Factor" by Cloud and Townsend, and "Always Daddy's Girl" by Wright. These books will be instrumental in helping you identify and deal with past issues that are affecting you now, helping you recognize your worth and understand boundaries. And lastly, they will help you in your relationships with family and the other loved ones in your life.

And remember, we truly aren't alone. We have our architect, our creator, who is our co-conspirator in this journey that has been mapped out for us. It's okay to lean on our architect. It's how it was meant to be.

So now that we have added exhale, take a step back, clear your mind, have some fun and be ready for new and refreshing ideas. And don't forget to excavate. Dig up and dig out all the "junk" in your life that has been holding you back. And don't be too proud to get the help you need!

Think like Albert Einstein who said something like this: *"The problems we have cannot be solved by the same level of thinking that created them."*

In other words, you can't see the forest for the trees, so you better go find someone with binoculars!

Next...

Are you finally feeling like the CEO of your life? Are your lungs filling up with fresh, clean air? Is every fiber of your body charged with inspired action? If so, it sounds like you are ready for some dynamic changes in your life. Get yourself in perfect position, poised like a panther ready to pounce. Lots of "p's" in that one – kinda like Peter Piper picked a peck of pickled peppers.

So take the plunge... here it comes!

Expand

I suppose this one sounds pretty logical, doesn't it? Expand your knowledge or expand your horizons. We've all heard these things before many times from parents and teachers. But I challenge you to look at this word differently today. Again we turn to Merriam-Webster. Expand: *"To open up, unfold. To write out in full* (not abbreviate), *elaborate, concentrate on the details, to enlarge."* Or, as I like to put it - to explore; to explore the possibilities and in doing so *effect* (change the outcome and end-product) and produce a new and unique result.

Hey, don't' abbreviate your life! Life isn't a tweet or a twitter! It is a poem, a beautiful sonnet, a snappy short story or maybe a grand novel – it's in the content. It's in the details and possibilities, and the way in which your life unfolds that is the glory of a life well lived. So let's get started and do some "effecting".

What is your story? What is your story up to now? Are you

satisfied with it? Obviously not, since you are reading this book. So, how do you want your story to read? If your story was written down and someone was reading it what do you think they would be thinking as they read? What would you want them to think or to feel? Have you been a Magellan or a Christopher Columbus? Or did you stay home and say, "The world is flat!" Did you take life at face value (who's face was it anyway) and not question or think for yourself? Did you make details matter, or did you think the small things were unimportant? Have you lived your life in such a way that others want to emulate you? Who would *you* want to emulate and why?

Elaborate your life. Spend time on every aspect of it and make it full of ideas and inventions, full of all sorts of people and adventures. Life isn't an appetizer! It's the "full meal deal." And it doesn't take too kindly to being abbreviated. And it doesn't take too kindly to being squeezed into a tiny box without holes to breathe, and then put up on the shelf to collect dust. It wants to fly. It wants to soar like the eagles and twinkle like a shining star. It wants to be full of color and light and displayed like an artist displays their creation at an art gallery. So whether your life is brand new, restored or remodeled, show it off. Fill it full of fearless fun! Jump on that zip-line and begin sailing over the treetops.

Okay, okay. All of this sounds motivating, but what does it really mean and how, on a practical basis, does one go about doing it? Here are some baby steps to take. First, take a brutally honest look at your life and write down what you see. Don't be afraid, it won't be all bad. What is different about your life compared to those exciting people you've read or heard about, and secretly wished you were? Pay attention to what you identify as the differences because the excuse can't be, "Oh I am so boring and so-n-so is so amazing and inspiring and motivating."

That one won't work, because even a slug is inspiring and motivating, especially to another slug. But it can be to you too! I have never met a discontented slug; they know how important they are. They eat and clean up the environment, and when they have accomplished that, they become a vital part of the survival and food chain. Their mission is to sacrifice their lives for the better good – they know their importance and don't take it for granted or get confused about it. They have embraced their destiny and they intend to be the "best" slug possible. They are realizing their *full slug potential* and they are proud of it!

I know I have said this before, but I will say it again, be present in your own life. Be intentional, live intentionally, purposefully and breathe in every detail. Feel every moment; savor it, make it a buffet. Then watch the movie "Auntie Mame." I think everyone on earth should have to watch this movie once a year because we tend to forget and let things slip away if it's not in front of our face often. I think everyone should have to watch "Pollyanna" every other year, too. Both of these movies have "seize the moment" and "make it count" as their headline. "Fear not!" The architect's got your back. Remember him? He designed you with greatness in mind, and with "full potential" written all over you. So what are *you* going to do about it?

Yes, what about you? Next, take that list you made and underline or circle your potentials, those talents and attributes you believe you can expand and expound upon. Then cross everything else out. We are just going to work with the potentials. Now, where the blanks are, fill in what you want to be, what you want to do, what you want to have, and how you want others to see you. Make sure you fill some of the blanks with things that excite you. The things that make you tingle all over, feel butterflies in your stomach, or put a big smile on your face. These are your "passionate" items and these are r-e-a-l-l-y important. You must pay close attention to them. Again, these are probably things you don't think you know how to do or have the resources for. They are things that seem too big or too lofty to try. These are things you are afraid you can't accomplish. Things you might fail at. These are things that you think others might scoff at you for or try to talk you out of doing, which means you *must* do them - for they most likely are part of your purpose.

Grab hold of every opportunity and look at your day as bucketfuls of small chances to make a difference in someone else's life. This is a "key" point. You have to get out of yourself, your selfishness, and your "How is this going to affect *me?*" way of thinking. Put someone else first! Before you know it your life has more meaning and "feels" bigger than it did before. Because it *is* bigger than it was before!

When you change you can't help but affect others. You can't help but change the lives of others. It's a domino effect and you are the catalyst that starts the first domino to fall (in a good way). Donate your time, talents, and energy to a charity and see the sky open up for you. Literally, a gentle rain of compassion and fulfillment will fall on you along with a generous portion of humble pie. When you realize how full your life already is and then, you heap on a big helping of "lending a hand of support" to someone else – Woo-wee! Look out! All of a sudden you are able to do things you never thought you could.

At the end of each day you should be tired. I don't mean you should be tired because you worked all day, and you did all those duties you had too. I mean you are exhausted from living every moment of that day like it was your last day. Think about it. What if today was your last day on earth? The last day of being a living, breathing flesh-covered human body on this earth. What would you do different? What would you say different? And who would you say it to? What would you make important and what would you let go of? Don't procrastinate your life! That is really a pet-peeve of mine. It really bugs the heck out of me. In fact, it makes me extremely mad. Procrastination is a bad word. And usually we procrastinate what we really need to do. Why? What is your trigger for procrastinating? Fear of failure? Fear of looking stupid? Maybe fear of responsibility? Or is it the fear of success? Hmmm... Now that's an interesting one.

You might think why would anyone be afraid to succeed? This one has been a little difficult for me to understand too. But I have come to realize, there are reasons why it is almost impossible for some people to succeed and here's why. They have been told since they were young that they were failures, they are worthless, they are nothing and they are stupid. So now they have incorporated those ideas into what they believe about themselves. And as we have already learned, we are what we believe; it is how our brain was made to work. If we believe we are failures then we have to make sure our belief system about ourselves comes true - so we will make sure we don't succeed. How? Well, there are many ways to make that happen; addictions, destructive behaviors, negative relationships, skipping classes and not studying so you fail, not showing up for an important appointment or reporting off from work until you get fired, just to name a few. All of these are examples of sabotaging yourself in some way.

Another reason someone may not want to succeed is that if they did, they might have more responsibility *or* get less attention or sympathy from someone. Possibly the only way they got attention as a kid was when they did something wrong. So now by being "good, right or successful" they fear they won't get what they *need* most, attention, at any cost.

Again you need to use that *examine* word and seek out if you have any of these procrastination pitfalls. Are you a failure "junkie?" Well, you better kick that habit or you are lying to yourself and not really wanting to change. Are you always buying books or tapes and reading articles about "changing your life" but never doing it? Aha!

Who are you fooling? It must be yourself because I bet others already know the "real" about you. So it's time you got *real* with yourself, get off that pitty-pot and change!

Wow, I got a little heated there! It's a soapbox of mine. I want to see you reach your full potential. It is important to me. It is what makes *me* tingle and feel the butterflies, a-fluttering. So, let's go back to that "big" life of yours. Just by you excepting the possibility of change, you are changing. So there you go! Do it *all* the way, embrace! Remember:

Embrace – Examine – Engage – Envision – Exhale – Excavate - Expand

Are you beginning to feel your voice? Do you hear a whisper of that something inside trying to be heard? That's it. That's your voice. As the Chief Executive Officer of your life, you have to have one, a voice I mean. And that voice needs to be strong so it can be heard and paid attention too. So it can be heard above the din of everything else that is making noise out there. To change your life you must find your voice. It's the inner voice, one that guides you, helps you maneuver through life. But it's more than that. Your voice is your platform, what you believe and what you believe is important in life.

What you are willing to stand up and shout at the top of your lungs for. What you are willing to risk alienating a friend or family member for. What you are willing to lose a job over. What you are willing to give up. And what are you willing to give away? Your voice is your price tag, your worth. What are you worth? What is your price tag? What can you be bought for or sold for? What are you willing to back down for?

Who are you today? Are you the same person no matter who is around and what is happening? Or are you a "changeling" depending who is in listening distance? What is your value and what are your values? This is your voice and as you expand you have to decide *who you are*. Who are you?

One more thought about expand before we move on. *Expand* means to open up, to conquer. Let me speak from a personal experience. Since I was young I have been afraid of water. I mean I go into the water, say a pool or the ocean. But I can't stand to get my face wet and I panic if my feet aren't touching the bottom and somehow my face gets under water. My mom was afraid the same way and I think she instilled this in me at a young age. I have tried many times to overcome this, and to some extent I have, but I can't say I am fully relaxed or even enjoy water activities.

About ten years ago I decided I was going to do something bold about my fear, so I went white water rafting and parasailing. What? Both of them at the same time? Not exactly, but close, within a few months, I did both.

The first one I tried was white water rafting. It probably is a good thing I really didn't know what it was going to be like because I wouldn't have done it. But, I called and made a reservation. At the time I told the person on the other end of the phone that I didn't know how to swim. They said, "No problem, you will have a life jacket plus there will be a staff on the raft with you."

Okay. The day arrived. I paid my money and again told the girl behind the counter "Now remember I don't swim." Again I was assured about the life jacket and the staff on the raft. Okay. I put my life jacket on and proceeded to march down to the rafts with the rest of the "raftees" and before I got in the raft I said, "I don't swim." Again they assured me, "No problem, just slide to the bottom of the raft." Okay. We are now in our rafts and the person sending us off, laughs and then proceeds to makes this announcement:

"And as an added bonus today we are starting your trip down river with an exciting feature. You will be going over a 12-foot waterfall and dropping below into the white water of the Chattahoochee River!"

I almost swallowed my tongue! I couldn't breathe. And I couldn't speak. Which probably was best because I wanted to scream, "Stop!" and jump out of the boat, I mean raft. I did survive, barely. I didn't have a heart attack. I didn't die – even though it felt like I was going too. All I did was fall to the bottom of the raft and once we hit bottom, I pulled myself back up and sat back on the raft. I did spend several more moments on the bottom of that raft, but pretty soon all I was paying attention to was the gorgeous scenery and beauty of the river. It was September so the leaves were changing. It was serene and peaceful and *hard work*. We had to paddle and squeeze our butt cheeks and legs to hold onto the side of the raft, but it was worth it. And at the end I really felt like I had accomplished something important. And I had, for me. I had taken charge. I was in the driver's seat. Power had been taken away from my fear. It felt great!

The parasailing came several months later and was much easier for me to do. I good friend of mine and I had gone to

Treasure Island, Florida for a few days as "beach bunnies". She had taken me to a Salvatore Dali museum (she is so interesting like that), and then we soaked up some sun on the beach. The last day we were there she talked me into the parasailing. It was pretty cool – flying through the air like a bird and *above all that water.* I survived and again felt powerful! I still have a picture of me with my parachute hanging on my office wall. A gentle reminder, "There is nothing to fear but fear itself" So face it! Face your fear. It really will change you. But only *you* can choose to do it. And only you can prevent it from happening. Which will you choose?

Would you choose?

Eecckk!?

Is *eecckk* even a word? I'm not really sure but I am sure of what it means to me. *Eecckk* represents all the stuff: things, people and circumstances that I need to stay away from or get out of my life because they are bad for me. It's one of those words that when you encounter it you run the other way and scream "*Eecckk*!" If life was a movie "E*ecckk"* would be the Wicked Witch of the West, Dr. Lechter and the shark from "Jaws" all rolled into one. It is rats, snakes and hairy spiders chasing me (that's mine). What's yours? Get a mental picture of the things that make your skin crawl, or what you are really "a-scared" of. Can you see them? Can you picture them? Can you feel them? Don't even entertain the thought that this is a silly exercise. This is important! Just do it!

Make it vivid. Taste it and feel it in the pit of your stomach. Are you ready for the next step? Okay, once you have this really powerful image stamped on your brain, click it. Snap it! Hit the save button because you need to store it in your computer of a brain and then have the ability to retrieve it when you need it. And when is that? When will you need it? It is every time you are about to enter the "run like hell" zone. You know the zone I am talking about. It's the zone when your "something is wrong but I can't help doing it" antennas go up. The zone where it feels like the hair on your arms and on the back of your neck are all standing up at once even though you can't see it happening, that zone. It's the zone of no return, that zone of lost incomes, broken hearts and near fatal injuries.

And it's the zone you need to stay out of and away from. So having the ability to conger up that *"eecckk"* image is critical to your success in saving yourself volumes of pain, stress and sleepless nights. So take some time and work on getting really good at perfecting your *"eecckk"* image and then when you are ready we will move on.

Next, put down this book.

No really, I mean it. Put this book down and go work on doing what we were just talking about. Go develop your escape button – your *"eecckk* icon!"

La, la, la...hum......... (This is me, waiting for you).

Again, I am waiting, patiently...

Okay, you better be ready since you have picked this book back up and are reading it again. This step has to be more than intuition. It has to be more than a guess, dumb luck or an "inkling". It has to be a distinct part of your total self. One that you have carefully developed and purposefully crafted and taken very seriously, just as you have with all the things you have thought were important in your life up to this point. To bring home this point, let's take a little trip down memory lane. Sometimes you have to go back and take a step backwards before you can take a giant leap forwards. This is one of those cases.

Get out a piece of paper and a pen. Oh no, not another list! "Yes, another list - an extremely important one." I want you to close your eyes and think of the things that you have done or the things you have let into your life that have brought disaster in some way. Think of all the things that you have attracted into your life that have been disastrous. Me? You mean I have attracted the very things I didn't want? Yes! That is why this section is so important. It is not always the obvious, but the subtle, why we keep repeating the same mistakes over and over again. We must be able to recognize the danger *before* we find ourselves marooned on that deserted island alone with three very hungry lions.

So let's continue on with your obvious list of disasters: dating or marrying the wrong person, buying the lemon of a house/car/investment, stealing, loaning money to the wrong person, too much drugs/alcohol/sex, and the big one - still being in one of those situations long after you know it's a problem.

Now, next to each one of the identified things on your list

write down how many times you have done it. That's right. Don't act so innocent. I know that you have done each of those things more than once because, it is extremely rare that we learn the first time from our mistakes. It usually takes making the same mistake over and over, letting the brick wall hit us again and again, before we are bruised enough and our brains are scrambled enough to *change*. Change our behavior and our choices.

Does it seem that déjà vue is a regular part of your life? That you are in the midst of a bad situation or a nasty relationship and you say to yourself, "Self, how did I get myself into this same mess *again*?" Does it feel like the same play keeps running over and over in your head and the same personality keeps showing up in your life, the one you hate or are intimidated by? The one you can't confront? These are all part of the *"eecckk"* factor.

There are two solutions to this problem. You can really take the time to identify what you need to stay away from, and at the same time you can work on dealing with what you have avoided dealing with so the same "bad seed" will quit showing up to wreak havoc in your life. Again, this is all up to you and takes work. If you don't want to work, then your life will not change and the "déjà vues" and "beastie personalities" will continue to haunt you over and over again. Your choice...

If you are still reading then you have chosen to work hard, so let's go. You have identified the people, situations and relationships that are toxic to you and now you need to look for patterns. Have you had a string of relationships and break-ups or divorces and it seems like it was the same person with just a different face? Have you had more than one person that you have let into your life that has abused you physically, mentally, emotionally or sexually? People who have controlled your every move and stopped you from being yourself and from doing things you wanted to do? Were they out of your life for a day or two or a week and you felt relieved, like you had been let out of prison? Has there been more than one of these situations in your life?

Have you made a new friend or hired a new employee and all of a sudden they are the "monster from hell" and you are stuck with them and you must figure a way out? Have you ever found yourself in a dangerous situation? Has it been more than once? If so, is it because you couldn't stand up for yourself and say "no" to something or someone, and now you feel this panic in the pit of your stomach and you want to run and hide but can't?

Have you gained and lost, and gained and lost large amounts of weight and find yourself eating a bag of doughnuts, three Big Macs or several boxes of KFC, a big Slurppie and then wolfing down a handful of Hershey Bars and Kit Kats? Do you have every size from 4 to 24 in your closet? And do you avoid looking in mirrors - except very late at night in the dark?

If you have said *yes* to any of the above, or felt a little guilty because you have done things very similar to these examples, your internal security button is broken. Or as I used to tell the ladies in our program, "Your picker is broken." That's right. I believe we all have an *internal knowing* that helps us make healthy choices. This internal knowing helps us make choices that keep us safe and secure. But when that internal knowing has been damaged for some reason other things start to make decisions for us. What other things?

Well, if you are between the ages of 12 and 50, hormones. I am mostly talking to the women now, but men aren't immune here. Hormones will make you do really stupid things if that "picker" inside you isn't working right. You will find yourself being attracted to "bad boys" (or girls) again and again. You might even marry one or two. They will make you feel bad about yourself, they will reject you or worse still, their *picker is* working perfectly, and they have zoned in on *you* because they know you will do *anything* for them.

Maybe it's a certain look they have, or they are the exact opposite of what your parents want for you or approve of. Maybe it's to get back at your parents or your ex. Guess what? Your picker is broken! It may be broken a little or it may have been demolished, either way, something is wrong. And if you think good is boring or dating someone who is good to you and will do anything for you is way too boring, *"broken."* Darn it! If they are responsible, hard working and respectful to everyone and you're not attracted to them because you think that's boring – *"b-r-o-k-e-n."*

Lastly, if you have the need, an overwhelming obsession, to fix and change people, especially the ones others have tried to fix and failed to, *"broken."* You can't fix or change anybody.

They need to do that for themselves. I could go on and on with examples but I think you get the picture.

You have to take yourself into the repair shop and get fixed. Yes, just like a car. You get the oil changed and tires rotated on your car don't you? If your tires are bald you get new ones, right? If the engine light comes on you take it to the mechanic to get it checked out, correct? Why? It is because we have been taught, "If you don't do regular maintenance on your car you will get a flat tire or break down on a back road somewhere." Well, guess what, you are like your car. You need regular maintenance and an occasional overhaul. If you don't get it you'll be stranded, all alone, in the dark somewhere along your road of life and you've forgotten to renew your AAA.

So after you've made your list and identified your patterns, it is now time to do something about them. You must fix your picker so your inner knowing is automatically (ha, ha, ha – "auto", get it?) making right choices for *you* and your internal security can keep you safe and healthy. Something here that is very important. It is crucial that you admit it. You have to acknowledge it. You can't run and you can't hide from it anymore. You really can't out run or out hide your problems or broken parts anyway, mainly your picker. I know you have heard before that you can't run away from your problems. You also can't hide from them either, because since they are usually already hidden they will pounce on *you* when you least expect it. So you must go hunt them out and conquer them yourself *first* before they get you!

It may be as simple as training your mind to pay close attention to certain warning signals that spell imminent danger for you. Practice this daily, make it an important part of your routine, and soon it will begin to become natural for you – automatic. Once that happens, you are well on your way to resetting your internal security button, your inner knowing. Then, Presto! Change-o! No more broken "picker"!

Some of you may have deeper issues and deep scars that can't be fixed so easily. You may need professional or pastoral counseling and an accountability partner to help you deal with the past. Help you reframe, recognize the positive in yourself, and learn to walk in victory as a fully healthy individual. The books I had mentioned earlier will be a must for you to identify your need for mental, emotional, physical or spiritual healing.

Whatever you choose to do - be determined and do it. Don't quit! Don't get side-tracked. There may be those who try to talk you out of making better choices and becoming free. They may try to put obstacles in your way of success. Don't let anyone stop you from being all you can be and reaching your full potential! You have an ultimate purpose here, remember? It's important. *You are important!*

This brings up another important issue, the people and things in your life that are pessimistic and influence you to be pessimistic and negative. You must get rid of them. Whether you physically kick them out of your life, kick them to the curb. Or rise up and ignore them, it has to be done. You will never succeed in mastering your life if you are walking around in doom and gloom with a black cloud over your head all the time. Remember all these *words* we have talked about so far are *action* words. Verbs are the grammatical name for them. They do not happen outside of you. They take action by *you* to work.

You must *honor yourself.* If you don't honor yourself, no one else will honor you either. You are worthy of being honored. Our architect did not make you to be dumped on. So don't think it is okay and let it happen to you. And don't sabotage yourself, remember? Even if you think you are a diamond in the rough, hey - you're a diamond, right? That means you are valuable, beautiful and special. You sparkle!

I want to elaborate on the word "reframe" for a moment. Many things happen to us and we do many "not-so-nice" things to others *and* to ourselves. We can't beat up ourselves and beat up others the rest of our lives. We have to get to a point where we can truly let go, forgive, reframe and possibly even find a small iota of humor in the reframing. By doing this we are rewriting our past to save our future. Repeat that out loud to yourself: *"I am rewriting my past so I can save my future."* That is a powerful statement! Really take time to think about it.

Your brain is an incredible instrument; a phenomenal gob of synapses, dendrites and electrical charges orchestrating your every move and thought. This delicate organ is also as tough as nails and has the ability to forget and hide things from you that are too monstrous to bear. It can trick you into believing that a lie is the truth and a truth is a lie and then store those memories until you die. It then can guide you through these memories or these "forget-eries" and the emotions that they stir up which now have become your current behaviors, actions and reactions.

Sounds complicated doesn't it? Well, these handfuls of trillions of brain cells are intricate and complicated, but at the same time are very basic and simple. The simplicity is: you can change your brain. That's right! You have the power to change what you think and how that thinking affects you. And in doing so make sure your future does not repeat the mistakes of your past. You can be free! Not only able to dream big, but to *accomplish* those big dreams!

Let me give you an example from my own life. When I first met my second husband Tom, he was deep into drug addiction. I didn't know it until I was already madly in love with him. It took many years, much forgiveness, and a tremendous amount of hard work on his part, but he conquered his addictions. He became an ordained minister and has helped many people change their own lives. But in the beginning while in his addiction, he was a "user and a manipulator".

I was his enabler. As a result, I went through many heartaches and misery. And boy did I blame him for it! Not only that, I went around telling everyone all the terrible things he had done to me. It got so bad that no one wanted to talk to me because all I did was repeat the stories over and over again of how he had wronged me. My life was out of control and I blamed him for it!

I was even making myself miserable. I wanted to get rid of me. I just couldn't shut off the record in my head, the "He did it to me!" record. Then I ran slap-dab into Al-anon. For those who don't know what that is, it is: "You are an enabler, you can't fix or change him, and *you* did it to yourself, quit blaming him" support group.

The day I realized this I got so mad, I threw books across the room. In fact, I threw anything that I could pick up across the room. I screamed and yelled. I cried and I got furious. How dare it be *me!* How dare someone think that it's *my* fault? Aren't I, the victim here? Shouldn't everyone feel sorry for me? Haven't "I" been the one victimized, depleted and controlled?

This went on for about a week. Then one morning I woke up and knew it was true. Wow, what a revelation! Did I feel stupid! Wasn't I a stupid idiot or what? I was a fool. I was a dummy. The list goes on and on. I beat myself up pretty good for about a week. One day out of the blue, I accepted it. I just accepted it. I wasn't a stupid idiot. I had made bad choices and I was the one responsible for those bad choices because I could have said "No" instead of saying, "Yes". I had the power. I *have* the power! I took responsibility for me. That was critical for me. *And it is critical for you.* Until responsibility is taken your brain can't put the proper actions into place for *you* to make the "next right choice".

I realized I had learned a big lesson. I had gone to the school of Farah. In fact, I had a Master's Degree from the Farah College. It was an invaluable education and I needed to put that invaluable education to good use. I had been able to take an honest look at my life of the last few years, reframe, turn it into a positive life experience, then use it to propel myself into a future of optimistic opportunities - endless opportunities. In fact, I went a step further. I begin to laugh. Not laugh at myself because I was stupid, but laugh because it was funny. And let me tell you, there were a lot of funny stories.

I'll share a short one with you. About a month after all this happened, it was springtime and the grass was getting high in the yard. I thought to myself, "This weekend I really better get out there and mow that grass." I walked into the garage and realized where there used to be a brand-new, shiny lawn mower there was a big gaping hole. It immediately hit me! Tom had pawned it to get money for drugs. At the same time I was thinking this, I was laughing. I was laughing out loud and the louder I laughed the better I felt.

I had the opportunity a few days later to talk to him; we were estranged at this time. I asked him about it. He said, "Did you just realize it was gone? I took it weeks ago." Again, I just couldn't stop laughing. My picker, my inner knowing and internal security button, was on the mend. Over the next months I would laugh about many things, and the humor and laughter helped to heal me. What they say is true, "the best medicine is laughter."

So, how about you? Can you do it too? Can you reframe, readjust, and move on? You must, or else there will be no freedom for you. Don't forget, you are not alone. You have your architect, the co-creator of your life, who is there to help, console and lift you up. He will carry you on his shoulders. Don't forget to call on him and use his help.

One last thought. It is okay to say "No" to others and "Yes" to yourself. You must! It is not written anywhere that you have to say "yes" to everything that is asked of you. Add "No!" to your vocabulary and use it regularly. Think of it as fiber or roughage (this ought to be a good one). Why? Because it helps you rid yourself of unwanted garbage, the poop of life!

So, now that you've have gotten rid of the "poop" in your life, it's time to pour in the "good stuff". You certainly have made plenty of room for it! And our next word please:

Endorphins

Endorphin is a noun and it is also a peptide and a natural pain killer in your brain. It blocks pain by mimicking a morphine-like substance. What does that mean for you? Simply put, it is something that blocks the bad or negative by substituting good or positive things in its place. I like that. This is definitely in line with what we have been talking about so far. But we are going to do a little twist on this noun today and use it as a verb, an action word, actually an action phrase; "etching out your endorphins, discovering your endorphins". In this section we will be talking about learning how to elevate your endorphins to a level where they can positively change the experience you are currently having.

An example of this might be: you have an obligation you must fulfill but it is going to be extremely difficult for you to do. There can be many reasons why. The reason it not important, what is important is that you are dreading it. Because you are dreading it, you may be depressed, sad, angry and anxious. All of this is decreasing your ability to succeed at what you must do. It sounds like you are in a no-win situation or lose-lose situation with no way out. So what is the solution? Is it possible to change the experience and change the outcome for yourself?

The answer is yes. I believe it is. But first we must do the work and identify your endorphins, so when you need them they will be readily available to you. Let's begin by closing our eyes. Don't peak! Next I want you to relax and start to think back and remember occasions or things that you really enjoyed. These must be ones that you really enjoyed, not just ones you liked or thought were okay. These things must be sensational and they must have left you highly charged in some way; excited, energized, fulfilled, feeling loved and cared for, or inspired and motivated. I think you get the idea. As you are remembering, it is important that you put yourself back in that situation and feel the feelings. Visualize it is happening right now. Feel it. Hear it. Smell and taste it. This embeds the experience into your memory vault, so to speak.

After you have done this for a while begin to write down these experiences. Again, this is a list, but a different kind of list. You are lining up your bullets, your "ammunition," so when needed, you can quickly pull them out and defend yourself.

These will be your defenses against the sad, the worrisome and the mundane of life. Your defenses will help you elevate your experience to the next level, take you to a new place, so you can have a heightened positive experience and accomplish what you thought impossible.

Let me share a personal example with you. Currently, while writing this book, I am working as a nurse three days a week on the 7pm to 7am shift. It is quite difficult for me physically and emotionally. But it pays the bills which is what I need at this time. On my days off I feel almost "normal" but, when I wake up the morning of my next work day I fell depressed. My body aches and sometimes even a feeling of dread comes over me. In the beginning, I was able to view my circumstances as a way to encourage and help the patients and the staff – letting God, my architect, work through me. But as months have worn on this has become increasingly difficult for me. It has become very difficult to keep this positive point of view.

After I let myself sit on the pity-pot for awhile I finally decided I had enough. I did something. I got out my meditation audio-tapes and my Andrea Bocelli CD's. Each day on my way to work, an hour drive by the way, I listened to them. The meditation and visualization tapes helped me relax and harness my positive energy. Repeating out loud some positive affirmations helped me to see the bigger picture and my long-range goals. It worked! I went into work in a great mood, with energy, without dread, and the 12 hours went by faster and with less stress. That's not all. I was able to be that encouragement to the patients and the staff, the exact reason why I am there in that job at this time. I elevated my experience to a level that not only could I live with for those 12 hours, but I could be utilized in a positive way in the lives of others. Others noticed it too. I got asked why I was in such a good mood, "What happened to you?"

People will be drawn to you. They will want to be around you because you are helping to elevate *them* to another level. No one really wants to be depressed or sad or live in a state of dread. People want to enjoy life. You can help others reach their enjoyment level by living the "enjoyment" yourself.

Honor your soul. Listen to your heart, listen to remember. Remember to feed your soul first. If your heart and soul are not full, overflowing with what is good, good for you and for others - you can never make an impact in or on this world. You won't be able to help others because you can't even help yourself!

All right, do you have your arsenal ready? Do you have your list in hand and memorized? If the answer is yes, let's proceed. Oh, by the way let me share a few more of my bullets with you: getting a pedicure, walking in the woods or collecting sea shells on the beach. This is my line of defense, my first "go-to's" I keep handy to use whenever I need them.

Let's talk mindsets. You need a new one. Everyone needs a new one at certain points in their life. Why? It's because, our mindset gets "stinky" and unproductive. It keeps us stuck in the mud. It keeps us doing the same thing over and over with no better results. You know what that is called don't you? Insanity. Yup! That's the definition. Doing the same thing over and over again and expecting a different outcome. The reality is you must do something different to get different results. Activate your new mindset, your new way of thinking and new way of acting. So wipe the slate clean, clean out the cobwebs of your brain and get busy, remodeling.

Quit saying, "This is the way I have always done it" or, "I tried something different before and it didn't work." Times change, people change and it's time you change! You can't use a 1980's remote control with your new flat screen TV, right? It won't work. It can't work. Exactly, this is the 21st century, get with it! Let's move!

We are moving quickly to keep our momentum going. The endorphins we have been talking about fit hand in hand with our next "E" word:

Encourage

ENCOURAGE is in capital letters because it is just about the most important word of *all* these very important words. Pulling out our trusty Merriam-Webster dictionary again, we find encourage: *"To give someone hope, confidence or courage," "To urge somebody to do something, to motivate," "To assist something to occur or increase."* Some synonyms for encourage are: inspire, reassure, support, foster, help and nurture.

Say these words out loud: hope, confidence, courage, motivate, reassure, support, nurture and inspire. *Hope, confidence, motivate, nurture and inspire.* I don't think you can get any better than those five words right there. My heart wants to say them over and over. I love the way they roll off my tongue:

Hope Confidence Motivate Nurture Inspire

I'm in love with the word inspire. That may sound strangely odd to you but that's the best way to describe it. Because when you are "in love" with someone you feel like you can fly, you want to do anything and everything for them, and with them. You don't want to let them out of your sight. You want to tell the world about them. And you will defend them even when it doesn't make sense. You will overlook their flaws and their mistakes. You will also take just about anything they will dish out, whether they love you back or not. Does that pretty much describe the "in love" experience?

That's, how I feel about inspire. If you take those other four words and build on each one, like steps, inspire would be at the top. Inspire would be the shining star atop the Christmas tree.

So, what's the recipe and how does it relate to our word, encourage? You start with a cup of *hope.* Add some *motivation,* which in turn pushes up the *confidence* a notch. Don't forget to keep stirring. You *nurture* that a little and then suddenly *inspiration* appears shining so big and bright it practically blinds you.

Now let's look at our important word *encourage* in three distinct ways:

Encourage others - Encourage ourselves - Random encourage = Inspiration

Before we get started there is only one ground rule but it is a crucial one: Give yourself permission to be real. None of this will work if you are fake or if you try to fake it. This is no time to put on a mask and be someone else. No pretending to be perfect, no one is. No pretending you have never made a mistake, everyone does. No acting like you know everything, you don't.

You must be authentic. You must be free to be who you are. To share who you are and to love who you are. You can't be afraid that people will laugh at you or reject you. And you mustn't use the old excuse that, "Talking about it makes me feel guilty or depressed," No excuses! None! Revel in your own imperfection. That's right, revel in your own imperfection! Listen without judgment, to others and to yourself. Allow yourself to find out who you really are so *encourage* can exist. So *encourage* can thrive. So *encourage* can succeed!

If you must take a few minutes, a few days or a few weeks to "get real" please do it, then come back and start reading again. If you believe you are or you can be real, let's move forward.

Let's take a look at the most traditional encourage with the most traditional approach first, encourage others. I believe that's the one that pops into most of our minds when we think about the word encourage.

To kick things off, I want to admit something to you. "I don't know everything." Did you figure that one out already? It's true. Me, myself, as a person is limited. That is where inspiration and my architect "make up the difference". On my own alone, I can do very little. But with my creator, my co-creator, I can do things beyond belief. So here is my admission to you. I didn't get it. Yup, that's right. Someone who spends so much time thinking about and doing "encouragement" work missed it. What did I miss? "America's Got Talent". You know, the TV show. I tried to watch it for a few years and thought it was – well, dumb. Very short-sighted on my part, I know. Then a few weeks ago something changed. I changed. My husband was watching the show, he really enjoys it and has been trying to get me to sit still and watch it for a long time. I would always make up an excuse. But for some reason this particular night I decided I would make the effort and watch it with him.

Then it happened. An 80 year-old grandma singing a rap song she wrote, a father and daughter singing duo, a street dance performer and a 54 year-old high school teacher singing opera performed. They performed, cried, and made it to the next round in Las Vegas. And I finally got it! I listened to their stories and saw their tears of relief and joy and witnessed their dream come true. It was about making their dream come true. They did it! They made their dream come true. In the end they may not win the competition, but that's okay. It wasn't about the winning. It was about having the courage to live their dream. To realize it's never too late to have your day in the sun. We all have the need to leave a mark, "We were here". It's a deep, inherit need. By the end of the show, I was crying too. I suddenly had a new perspective. I was seeing it through new eyes, their eyes. It was truly inspirational!

This reality show, this competition, is able to provide a way for the average person to make their dream come true. They didn't have to be fabulous. In fact many are only fair and some, not good at all. For many being the best isn't their goal. Their goal is the dream. And their dream is to let what is inside of them out and share it with others. Why share it with others? Because that may just be the encouragement that someone in the studio audience or the TV audience needs to help them make *their own dream come true*. So throw away the fear and the self-consciousness like they did. And tell the story of you!

We walk around all day bumping into people, standing next to them in the bank, or sitting beside them on the bus and, we don't know their stories. We don't know their fears, pain and sorrows. We don't know their hopes and dreams. And we don't know their gifts and talents or their "special purpose". In fact, most of the time, we don't even see the people at all. We are so caught up in ourselves and our problems, we miss wonderful opportunities to meet and hear others' stories. We don't pay attention. We don't notice and we miss opportunities to encourage others and let others *encourage us*. We've missed the blessing.

Are we afraid we will be late? Don't we care about people anymore? Are we afraid they will hurt us or ask us for a favor? What is it that keeps us away from others? We weren't designed that way. We were designed to be social beings. And by social I don't mean we keep our heads down and glued to a computer or phone and do the tweet, twitter and email thing and believe that's real communication. All we are doing is communicating with a machine and luckily *the machine* passes on the words, and then delivers those words to a person on the other end that *it* is communicating with. We are missing the most important element, the *people* with their emotions, feelings, and human interactions.

Think about this and try it sometime. Send an email to your spouse or love-of-your-life and just say, "I hate you". If they read it as it is typed, they will think you hate them. Then they will automatically shoot you an email back and tell you they hate you too, call you a nasty name, or say something ugly about you. Now, if in all reality you don't hate them, in fact you love them. And if you were actually talking with them the laughter or "teasing" in your voice would have let them know that you were just telling them in a funny way that you loved them. But without the "human" element, the human voice and the touch of tone and emotion, you may end up getting a divorce.

That is why we must fight hard to remain connected with each other. Stay connected with the people we know and love, and the people we haven't met yet. Let serendipity happen every day. Talk to people, make the effort, they are everywhere. Strike up a conversation, discover their stories. You will be surprised and amazed how your life lines up with them in some way. How you can share an experience or give them a compliment that will make a difference in their life today. Test it out. Get a little notebook and for a week try to talk to as many people as possible. And *listen.* Many times people just need to be heard, to be validated. Just for someone to listen to them, for someone to take the time and give them their attention. That by itself could take their day from sad to glad.

Go a step further. Make it a point to decorate someone's life each day. Let them know they are doing a great job, or compliment them on how they look or how much you enjoyed the meal they made you. Realize that people have invested their time in cooking a meal or picking out a special card for you. Thank them, make them feel appreciated. Everyone wants to feel some acknowledgement for what they have done, or tried to do. Even the things that haven't turned out so great, it's the thought that counts. So you make it count and recognize the effort, express gratitude for their willingness to try!

Think of words like beautify, enrich, adorn and ornament. What pictures and emotions do they bring up in you? Good ones, right? Well that is what you want to do for others. Make them feel good, make they feel able, capable and worthy. Realizing they are worthy not only to dream their dream but to make their dream happen, see their dream become a reality.

Find out their dreams and aspirations. You will be amazed the people your architect will put in your path, the very people who you can encourage in some way, or who will inspire *you.* And what is the best endorphin for inspiring you? That's right, helping others. It's giving someone a hand, not a hand-out.

There is a big difference. When you give a hand-out there is a negative connotation attached to it. This undertone is that the person in some way is not worthy, they are less than. You don't give hand-outs! You give hand-ups! You give people a hand, a helping hand, a lift, a lift-up. The implication is now uplifting, positive, motivational and inspirational. You feel good and the other person does not feel bad. That is very important! You are not handing out a meaningless something here. You are changing lives, theirs and *yours.* And that is why you are reading this book, correct? *To change your life...*

You may have the resources to give someone a job, pay a bill, refer them to the right professional, encourage them to do something they always wanted or needed to do but were afraid. Or even the resources to forgive and *live.* When you don't forgive you die a little everyday, but when you forgive living begins again. You can literally gain back what you have lost. No better gift to give someone than to encourage and help them live their dream. You will change their life. They will change yours.

There are so many movies and books out there for you to investigate that will help you find your own courage to encourage. I am going to list a few of my favorites: "Rudy", "Secretariat", "Sea Biscuit" and "The Blind Side". In each one there is a pivotal moment where the intent and the hope collide with *your* soul, and "Niagara Falls" happens. You can't control it. It is truly uncontrollable. It's the "human" element, your humanness for humanity. It's wonderful. It is what separates us from the animals, the lions and tigers and bears.

Let this one bounce off you. Maybe we are just here to affect one person. Maybe our purpose is to be a catalyst in someone else's life. And if we miss it, we have missed our purpose. Does that bother you to think you are not here just for yourself, a spouse, child, best friend or job? That you are not here to have a big house, fancy car and a bunch of toys? Does it stun you to think you are here for someone else's dream or good fortune? Don't fret. You see helping others to realize their dream helps you make your dream come true too! Ponder that one for awhile. Let the pot simmer on that one for an afternoon. Let the embers on that one warm your heart today, and let it spill over into tomorrow and the handfuls of tomorrows.

Maybe the most important encouragement you can give someone else is kind words. Words can mend a broken heart or they can cut like a knife. And what is the key word in that first sentence? Go ahead and guess. Did you get it right? It's "give". That's right, we give encouragement. It's very simple, we give, we encourage. Kind and positive words, a hug, a smile, a thumbs-up or a gold star at the top of the paper, these things make others spirits soar. It makes them keep on trying, and keeps them wanting to try. It encourages them to try a little harder and a little longer, to not give up. Hey, give the man dying of thirst a drink of water for Pete's sake! Hurry!

Take a chance. Get of your comfort zone. Pretend you are someone else doing it if you have to the first time. And once you do it and it works, you will be hooked! You will want to do it everyday. Hey, that is pretty close to a line from the movie

"Scrooged". Boy that is another movie I really like. It is proof that even the most selfish person, if properly inspired, can be an inspiration. No one is exempt. No one is beyond redemption. So if you are saying to yourself, "I am not an encourager." Quit it! I don't believe you. You are an encourager! You can encourage. You will encourage. So go and encourage. Be a part of something awesome and spine-tingling. Maybe someday someone will write a book about you, you never know. That's the exciting part. You don't know. The possibilities are endless. What a world it would be if we were all encouragers. What if every day encouraging was going on all around the world? Boy, wouldn't that be something?

Okay, let's talk about a few more examples of encouraging others. Do you ever do someone else's job or them? How about holding a door open, or paying for someone's groceries, complimenting someone on how they look or what they are wearing? My mom used to carry around chocolate kisses and chocolate hearts with her all the time and just give them out to people, randomly. People lit up like Christmas trees! Just a simple gesture like that touched people immensely. People smiled, they struck up conversations, they laughed and they ate the candy. It didn't cost much and it was something she liked to do, because she *l-o-v-e-d* chocolate, almost as much as me. Hey, maybe that's where I got it from. Ya think?

We have all been told that the most important phrase you can say to some one is, "I Love You". Poems have been written about it, movies have been made around this theme, and women everywhere wait around to hear it and swoon when they do. But I beg to differ with this trend. I think the most life-changing phrase you can say to someone is, "I Believe in You". Love can be blind (deaf and dumb, too) but to be believed in and for someone to say, "I believe in *you*" takes thought and effort, and the willingness to engage with that person. It just doesn't come from a hormonal or a chemical reaction.

It also implies that you are accepting them as they are now. They are acceptable, warts and all. Now you may be not only looking at them as they are but are probably seeing them in your mind's eye as you believe they can be. Again that example of a diamond in the rough: the unpolished diamond that just needs a little spit-shine. You are looking at them through the eyes of encouragement. The art of encouraging, truly a fine art. Take some time and create a little.

A small side-note from a day in my life: For years I have wanted to learn to paint. And for a long time I didn't think I could or should paint without lessons. Well, I realized am not breaking the law if I paint without lessons. I mean I won't go to jail, I won't get arrested. Not unless I hit someone over the head with one of my paintings.

Anyway, I bought some paints, brushes, 8 x 10 canvases and started to paint what I saw from my back porch, nature in all its glory. I had been working on it for a few weeks and just happened to stop in at a local framing and art shop. They display local artist's work for sale along with the framing they do. I was having difficulty with the mountains I was trying to paint and was hoping for some advice. The mountains are so gorgeous around here and mine on canvas looked artificial. I brought my painting in and was admiring all the paintings hanging on the walls. After a while I began talking with the proprietor about my struggles. He said he couldn't draw a stick figure but why didn't I ask the fellow in the next room as he was an artist. He had several paintings on display there and gave art lessons in Asheville. So for the next fifteen minutes I got a spontaneous lesson from the artist who was only too glad to share some pointers with me. He even told me I had put together some nice colors in my painting and said, "Never to lose my naivety, as it can be my best asset."

After my errands, I came home, took his advice and in less than twenty minutes my mountains became real and my painting took on a whole new look. What happened? What happened was I gained more than the knowledge he was giving me. I gained confidence, validation and joy, the joy of being capable and creating. It spontaneously became more fun and natural for me and not just something I was trying too hard to do. I was doing it naturally and it made me feel good.

He encouraged me.

Your assignment if you so choose to accept it: Go out and encourage everyone you meet. Keep a journal of what happens. Take snapshots in your mind, scrapbook them, and pull them out when you need a reminder of how good it feels to make a difference in someone else's life. Go, go, go! Do, do, do! Practice, practice, practice! I'll wait. I'll wait for you until you are ready for the next step.

Zzzzzzzzzzzzz...

Oh, you back so soon...?

I was just taking a little siesta with my feet up, a tall glass of ice tea, enjoying the cool breeze and the setting sun. Alas, let's get back to work. Now comes the difficult part, encouraging yourself. Did you know you can't wait for encouragement? We all have to know how to encourage ourselves. We all have been doing a form of this most of our life. We just didn't necessarily call it encouragement. There are a lot of other names for it: "Don't cry", "Keep a stiff upper lip", "Smile", "Try and try again". The list can go on and on. And depending in what era your parents were born, may dictate the jargon.

So we are not totally in the dark when it comes to this process, but it is important that we tweak our brains a little to get a new perspective, and begin to get the maximum effectiveness for the success we want. So let's pull in the strays, make a circle, stoke the fire and sit a spell because we are in for a long night.

Do you feel your life has been full of detours and roads under construction? Do you feel like you have been side-swiped by too many unmarked cars? And do you feel your tires have been flattened by too many potholes? Well, join the club, you are part of the human race and we all feel like that on any given day. But if we try to look at our life from the perspective that there are no mistakes (our architect hasn't made any). And that our life is a work in progress, only then we can begin to *seize the opportunity!* What opportunity are we supposed to seize?

We must seize the fact that we have a lifetime to accomplish our dream, our goal, and our ultimate purpose. The only catch is - we don't know how long that "lifetime" will be.

Pretty big catch, huh?

So what do we do?

We have to learn to believe in *ourselves.* We have to believe that there is nothing we can't do. We have to believe we don't have to be perfect, brilliant or a creative genius to try. We have to put aside the fear, put aside all the reasons we have told ourselves "we can't," and just go ahead and do it any way. Do it for the fun of it. Do it for the heck of it. Pretend you are a famous person who *can* do it and then do it.

And *know* you are not alone. Because you aren't! You didn't just show up on this planet by accident. Two planets didn't slam into each other and "poof" - out pops you. You had a creator, an awesome and amazing force that knew you and your purpose before you took your first breath. So even if at times you feel alone, you aren't. You have a partner who wants you to be fulfilled in your ultimate purpose and will go to any length to help you succeed, to mold your dreams into reality and accomplish it. And remember, the truth is the truth no matter whether you believe it or not. It is what it is. That's a good thing. Because if we had to rely on ourselves alone and on how we feel on any given day, we would be in heap of trouble.

We have to live each day to the fullest because it could be our last. We have to leave no apology unsaid, no comment unspoken and no encouragement not given. We have to love ourselves the way we are, or at least love the fact that we are here today and have another chance to make a difference. We have another chance to change our lives and start a chain reaction of change on this earth. Get excited! Ignite the fire and passion within yourselves. Think of yourself as "The Little Red Engine That Could" and say: "I think I can", "I think I can". "I know I can" "I know I can". And guess what? You can! You really can. Will it be perfect? Will it be 100% correct the first time? Maybe...

But that isn't what is important. What is important is you have harnessed the passion inside and redirected it to take that first step towards your dream. Every step after that is easier. So what if there are a few stones or rocks or boulders in your way. You can do it! You can go over them, around them or through them. There is nothing you can't do!

Hey, this is good stuff. You need to be saying this over and over again to yourself. Hello, encourage yourself through uplifting self-talk. Strengthen your resolve to the point that no one or nothing can stop you. No one can deter you from your mission, your dream, your path to your ultimate and divine purpose and calling. You have an undying spirit within you. You were born with this spirit. Life may have wounded you. It may have wounded you to the point where you don't feel or realize this undying spirit still is within you. But it is. Let it live. Let it breathe. Give it flight. Let it soar. Let is shine and overflow unto others. It's big enough and strong enough. And can't be stopped!

Look out world, here you come!

How do you feel? Are you pumped? Are you ready to conquer the world?

Great!

You are now ready for the third segment of our encourage trilogy. We have encouraged others. We have learned to encourage ourselves. And now we are ready to encourage with the objective of pure encouragement. Does that sound like something that might intrigue you? I hope so. What I mean is - we aren't encouraging a person. We are participating in pure encouragement by joining in and being a part of a cause, a movement, something greater than ourselves. And it is for the "whole" that we, by entering in raise the level of encouraging and create an expediential experience. Sound impressive? Well it is and then it isn't. It is, because many lives have been changed from such an occurrence. And it isn't, because it's not as complicated as it sounds. All you have to do is say, "no" or "yes" and mean it, and be willing to do what ever it takes to back up your statement. It's that simple.

I feel very fortunate to have been a teenager and in my 20's during the late 60's, 70's and early 80's. Everyone was joining in and marching: From civil rights, to saving the whales, to high gas prices, to pollution, to the Vietnam War, to women's lib. There was no lack of issues to get behind and raise conscience on. The music and movie industry had a field day with these causes. The songs and movies that came out in support of, or in protest against, changed the face of public opinion.

It seems a little sad that today we don't seem able to do the things we could back then. I don't know if it is because we have become a more global society, and what we do here in the U.S. just doesn't affect us, it has affect around the world. So the governments and economies of other countries are now involved and the power we had we don't have anymore. There is so much streaming in on us every split second that maybe it's too hard to concentrate on one cause very long. Something else comes to take our focus away. I guess that's it. The sole focus we used to have has now been replaced by thousands of sizzling sound bites bombarding our brains. I don't have the answer, just thoughts and questions. How do we make a difference in this group, the "whole," to elevate encouragement and make a stand for our cause and make a difference in today's world?

We must be intentional. We must be determined. And we must not give up. We can't throw in the towel even though we may not see things happening quickly enough for us. That's the curse of 21st century – hurry, hurry, hurry! And if we don't see results quick enough, we jump to something else. Hey, if we continue to do this, nothing will change. Well, that's not entirely true. Things will change, of course. But it may not be the way we want them to change because we are not getting involved. We are sitting on the sidelines just letting it happen. So this last part of the lesson for our word *encourage* is: fight and don't settle until you have seen the change you want. Remember, all things are possible and nothing is impossible. You must continue to believe and stay on course.

There are no limits except the ones *we* put on ourselves. Yes, we are the culprit. Our creativeness and possibilities are limitless. No walls can hold you. No bars can hold you. So stop struggling with yourself. The only struggle is, between you and *you.* The only person who can stop you, *is you!*

There are no physical boundaries just internal ones. And since this is true, then you literally are the CEO of your life. You are the captain of your ship, the master of your fate and the holder of your future - your dream, your purpose. In reality, *your reality,* hinges on only *you and the power of your mind.* So make your banner read, "I have the determination never to give up, settle or quit". Hold that banner high and wave it like a flag in the face of all that tries to stand in your way. Display that banner with pride and bold intention, and the humbleness of knowing your architect has given you everything you need to accomplish the task before you. You want for nothing. You have abundance of everything.

And don't' forget, – "It looks good on a resume".

Where did that one come from? You mean I am looking for a job and need a resume? Not exactly, I mean the resume of life, your life. There are some accomplishments, like your ultimate purpose, that can only be fully realized and fully embraced with a resume full of accepted opportunities through overcoming life's obstacles. Every time you add to your resume – it's your perseverance that transports you from novice to expert. You graduate from the high school of life to college, and as you boldly tackle what you are most afraid of, you attain admission to graduate school and beyond.

It may take some patience on your part. So be patient. The best is yet to come! There's time. Let's review for a moment before we learn about the last important word in this verb category. We've recently added:

Eecckk! **Endorphins** **Encourage**

Do you see how they fit into our plan? Are you beginning to see how with each addition we are escalating the power to change within ourselves? Are you ready for the finale, the climax to this overture?

Ready? Here is comes:

EMPOWER

If you guessed it, give yourself a "high-five" and an extra ten points.

Now empower is a remarkable word. As the definition dictates it not only gives power to and is powerful in itself but it also authorizes, it gives authority to, a double-dose of power. Just what is needed to change your life, right? So let's look at two separate uses for this all-important *empower.* First let's look at it by itself and pretend we have not just talked about ten other "E" words with their steps to a changed life.

Let's take a look at the Merriam-Webster Dictionary and see what it has to say about empower. Empower: *"To promote the self-actualization or influence of, to enable, to qualify."* You are seeking changes in your life that will empower you.

To empower someone is to give them the tools/knowledge they need so they have the power to make a change or do something new/different in their life. The same goes for you. You can allow yourself to be empowered to make a change, and have a future that is not the same as your past.

How do we empower others? How do we *allow* ourselves to be empowered?

Simply put, to give the opportunity and the power to others we must put them first for a minute. Take time to listen to them. Find out what they need to be qualified and to feel powerful enough to try something new, to make a change, or step out and take a chance. Don't be thinking you automatically know what they need or what they should do. You have to listen to what they are telling you, and what they are not telling you. Be sensitive. And just *listen.* Quiet your mind and your urge to talk, and listen not just with your ears but your mind and with your heart. Only then can you ever hope to help someone.

You may have the tangible; money, a contact, educational knowledge, etc... to help them. Maybe it's just the shoulder they need to bounce their hopes, dreams and ideas off of. But maybe it is being a mentor to them over time, which could last months or even years. Are you willing to make that investment in another person? The time and energy and patience it might take? I hope so. I bet someone has already done that for you and if they haven't, someone surely will in the future.

I don't think any of us make it through life without at least one "special person" who has seen a spark in us, and fanned that spark into a flame. I am a big-time believer in what goes around comes around. So, if you want someone to invest in you, you first must invest in someone else. You can't reap a harvest if you haven't sown any seeds and watered them. Get it? Hello, is anyone home? So get busy! The fastest way you can be empowered yourself is to be part of "empowering" someone else. If you don't believe that, I'm sorry but it's true. If you still don't believe it, don't just take my word for it, try it out. Try it for yourself. Try it to prove me wrong. I dare you!

Do you want some great ideas to get you started? Here goes. Look in the newspaper at the "needed" or "looking for" section. Here is where people post items or services they are looking for. You may have just what they need. Invest in them and make a difference. It's called volunteering, volunteering your services, your time or an item from your possession to theirs. Or you can put an ad in the paper yourself *offering* your services, your time or an item (again for free). Both these are great ways to meet, talk with, and help out someone else. Who knows, in the long run, you may be the one who gets helped the most. Think about it.

Another idea is to call the senior center or non-profit organization in your town and offer to volunteer. They are always needing help in the office or running errands. You may have the precise talent or gift that the participants need. And dare I say it? You will probably be the one who is blessed the most from this. Go through your closet and gather up all the stuff you haven't worn in years and donate it. Go through your pantry and cupboards, and gather all the cans, boxes and packages that have been gathering dust and *donate them*. Again you are helping, but also you are meeting some wonderful people and learning about some inspiring organizations.

Read the paper and see what events are coming up in your

area, call and donate your time, services or items they might need to make their event a great success. These are just a few ideas. I'm sure you can come up with many more. Try the schools, technical schools or colleges in your area. And hey, walk out your front door, turn your head to the right and then to the left. You have neighbors, don't you? Probably some of them are elderly or have limitations in some way. Knock on their door and offer to do something for them; cut their grass, clean out their garage, weed, trim and prune. When you go to the grocery store buy an extra quart of strawberries and give it to the family across the street.

Speaking of grocery stores, pay for someone else's groceries or help load bags of groceries into someone's car. Make a cake and give it to the new neighbors down the street, or better yet invite them over to your house for coffee and cake and sweet tea. All original or transplant "Southerners" love sweet tea. Okay, I think I have dosed you with enough, so let's move on.

If you are putting 2 and 2 together to make 4, then the progression of this book and the progression of your thinking must take us to the conclusion and solution that your sum = (equals) *empower.* Am I right? This is where our directions have been taking you, correct? You are trying to build a staircase to a destination that is your life changed. It's like "Stairway to Heaven". Whoops! No, that was a Led Zeppelin song. Boy that sure dated me, memories, huh? But seriously, it is like a stairway leading you to the top, the prize, the treasure – a life that exemplifies you. Wow-wee! I really like that "E" word, a lot!

A few questions to think about: What changes have you noticed in yourself and in your life since you started this adventure with me? How have your relationships changed with the people around you? How many “new” friends do you have now? How much baggage have you gotten rid of so far? What passions have been fired up? What longings are now surging through your body? Are you more confident? Is your life more stable or less stable? Do you wake up depressed and want to pull the covers over your head, or do you wake up with so much anticipation that you can’t wait to jump out of bed and see what exciting things the day will bring? Have you put any of this into practice or are you procrastinating? Are you still afraid or have you overcome your fears?

All valid questions...What were your answers? Be honest with yourself. It is great if you have begun to process and absorb what you have read so far. But, if you haven’t, don’t beat yourself up. That’s the whole point. Don’t beat yourself up! We are all a work in progress no matter where we find our self along the way. It’s a “road of life” but it comes without a Mapquest. And, as I hope you have learned, there are no mistakes, there are just “opportunities.” So don’t miss out on those. Take advantage of each and every one of them. It’s your life, no one else’s. It is what you make of it. And you can make the most of it. You can make it remarkable!

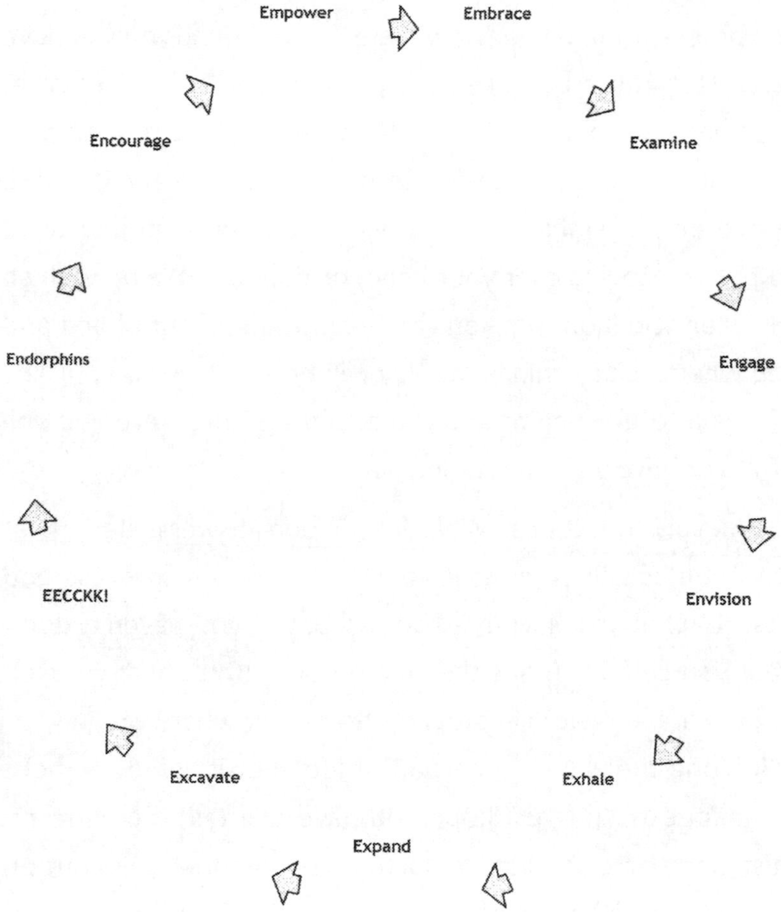

EMPOWER - The Road to <u>Empowerment</u>

As I promised we are going to talk about the other side of empower, the side that has "your" name on it. How do you allow yourself to be empowered?

Who has the authority to empower you? You! It's been you all along! Throw your pride out the window! Ask for help, we all need it now and again. Take a chance and be vulnerable. Let yourself be vulnerable. Believe it or not you won't break – you really are not that fragile. Open up and let others know the *real* you.

There is an important unspoken word, which is the invisible foundational piece holding empower steady and stable. That word, that concept, is trust. When you empower someone you trust them with what you are giving them. Whether it is tangible such as food, shelter or money, or it is intangible, such as the power for them to make their own decisions. You must trust that person with it. So what about you? Are you any less in need of trust than other people are? The answer is No!

If someone is giving you the tools you need for your empowerment, understand that they are giving you something worth much more, their trust. And trust is not something to be taken lightly. Since trust is not to be taken lightly, you need to trust yourself. Allow yourself to accept being empowered. It's a choice. There's that "choice" word again. You can decide to say, "Yes" to the trust, or you can decide to say, "No." Don't forget, not making that decision is still making a choice – it's the choice not to decide and let life do it for you. The result, you just lost what you gained. *You have lost your empowerment*!

I hope when you read the definition of empower you envisioned the word self-actualization. Self-actualization is a high goal to attain, and one our human spirit and soul strive to meet. Maslow, a true pioneer of Psychology, in his "hierarchy" puts it at the tippy top of the pyramid. He represents it as the final destination, his idea of treasure. For our purposes, it is the goal to your ultimate destination, your ultimate purpose. That is why it is the final spoke in our verb wheel. The culmination of all the "verb" work you must do to realize *change* in its entirety.

How are you feeling now? Have your thoughts gone in directions and into places they have never been before? Are you still as excited as I am to embrace more?

I hope so! Not only have you made great progress and learned some amazing lessons so far, you are now ready to embark on the next leg of your journey.

So was this first part the chicken or the egg?

Keep smiling, not only will it not break your face, but it will keep everyone guessing.

NOTES

Dream...

Dream big
Believe always
Trust unabashed
Love unconditionally
Shine eternally...

BE IT

To be or not to be...**that is the question**

I want to be a __________. How would you finish that sentence? Remember the game you played as a child? All standing in a circle and one by one blurting out what they wanted to be when they grew up.

In that circle, as innocents, we were all equal. As children we take everything at face value. There are no hidden agendas. We only learn that as we grow up. But in that circle equality was the code, it reigned.

So it seems appropriate that our first very important word under our "noun" or "To Be" category should be **equal** and its kissing cousin, **equality**. Let's start with some definitions of equal: *"Regarding or affecting all objects in the same way, impartial." "Like (same) in quality, nature or status." "Like (same) for each member of the group, class or society."* And some great synonyms are: unbiased, fair, unprejudiced, just and objective. Let's give a big round of applause to the Bing and Merriam-Webster Dictionaries!

So let's talk about what it really means to be an *equal* person, or a person of *equality.* First, why don't you tell me what you think it means and then we'll talk. Take a few minutes, think about it, then get a paper and pen and write it down. I'll wait.

"Whistle while you work"– tweet, tweet-tweet, tweet, tweet, tweet, tweet...

I believe you already have something written down on your paper so let's go ahead and begin. A person of equality would look at everything the same. By that, I mean they would be able to see all sides to an argument. They would be able to understand the points of view of all persons involved. If it was a topic, they would be able to view it as multi-layered and discuss the pros and cons. If they were a debater, they would be able to debate both sides equally. They would treat everyone the same in every situation. Even if one of the persons involved was a loved one or someone they disliked. Oh-oh, maybe if they were truly a person of equality they wouldn't dislike anyone. They would be able to disagree without the emotion or negativity of the disliking. What do you think?

An *equal* person would not judge another person, group or culture because of the way they looked, talked, acted or thought. They would never tell off-color jokes or make fun of people because that would be prejudice. Boy, they would make a great Miss America pageant contestant, wouldn't they? Maybe this is what we need when we pick a new president. We need to find a 100% person of equality and let them choose the right person. They couldn't be swayed by the commercials or the mud-slinging. They wouldn't be fooled by the "smoozing."

Do you think a 100% person of equality could be found? I don't know. I know many people do try hard, but are we humans truly capable of being 100% equal all the time? That really is philosophical and debatable.

Let's do an experiment you and I. Let's both take the next 24 hours and right down every time we are not being equal. Right down every time we are being prejudiced or unfair, not objective, or unjust. How big of a number do you think we would have? I say let's sleep for 24 hours and then it would be zero. That's the only time I think anyone would be able to get a zero.

I believe our human nature and being equal are always at odds with each other, and it takes being very intentional and diligent to not let our nature get the upper hand. We must fight. It's like having a little angel on your right shoulder and a little devil on your left, a constant struggle between doing "good" and "almost" doing good. Better still, let's say it's another one of those fighting situations where we must pay attention and be on guard, so we will do the right thing. It is so easy to slack off, be lazy and let things go over our heads. Again, we must always question and probe – be purposeful. Not think and act the way we do because our parents did, "It's the way I was raised" or, "Why should I care?"

We must care! Our future and the future of our planet depend on it. So get busy! Hey, have you every cut a cake and handed out a bigger piece to your friend or relative? What other things can you think of you have done similar to that? I bet there are quite a few. We all have done them. But is that being unequal? Maybe things like that don't matter? What do you think? Did you realize I was going to ask you almost as many questions as I was going to give you information? Hey baby, you got to work for it, life "ain't" easy.

Now I am going to challenge you with something else. We are going to discuss equal in a way we haven't discussed it yet. We have talked about you or us being equal, or having equality with others but, what haven't we talked about yet? You got it! *You!* Are you being equal with you? Are you bringing equality to the table with you when it comes to *you*?

Hmmm, hadn't thought about that one? Let that one sink in. Are you equal with you? Do you believe you are as good as everyone else, but not better than anyone else? Do you believe you deserve the same as everyone else, not better, but no worse? Do you believe that if you work hard you should get more? But then what about the person who is born disabled in some way and cannot work as hard as you? Do they deserve less? Do they deserve more? What exactly does equality really mean? Because there will always be people with different levels of health, wealth and creative resources. And how do we make things equal and balance everything evenly between people, culture, countries and personal beliefs?

I bet you never wanted to think this hard did you? Sorry, life "ain't" easy.

I don't know who first coined that phrase, but they sure were right. So what do we do?

It's crucial that we become as full of equality as we can. It's going to be a life-long process, but if we truly are going to change our life, we must try. Every time we catch ourselves being prejudiced, biased, or not being objective - we have to STOP, fix the situation, and not do it again. It's that simple. But have no doubt it will be hard work. You may lose some friends along the way. Are they friends if you lose them because you have become a person of equality and integrity? What kind of friend were they in the first place? On the positive side, you will gain friends. And I think these friends may be better for you anyway.

Now let's talk more about you, *and you*. Do you give yourself credit when you do the right thing, when you make a difference in someone's life or when you have acted unselfishly? Do you think you deserve a healthy body, a good job, a bank account and a loving, caring spouse who doesn't abuse you? There is an old adage that says, "You have to love yourself or no one else will". It's true you know. It you don't respect yourself enough to be equal, you have just given permission for others to treat you unequally. Does that make sense to you?

You have the power! If you don't feel that you do, then it is your job to develop your sense of power and realize you are equal. It is okay to take a few minutes for yourself, or buy yourself something new that makes you feel special. You are special in the same way that everyone is special. Take the time to look at yourself, take the time to look at others. Just take the time. Don't rush through your day, blink and its night. Blink again, and it's morning. Blink again and it's next year. Before you know it your week, month and year is gone and you have no idea where it went. Or what the heck you did during it! More importantly, what the heck do you have to show for it?

Let's take a test. First question: "How do you walk?" Do you walk with your head held high or with it down? Are your eyes open, bright and inquiring or downcast and dull? Is there a spring in your step? Do you have an air of authority? Or is it a hesitant shuffle? Are all your senses alert and ready to tackle what is coming, or are they dozing in hibernation? You can't be equal unless you walk, breathe, and live with equality, and in equality. Forget superiority and inferiority. You have no right to be either one of those. Let that one sink in. You have *no right* to be either one of those. That's right. Your architect drew up the plans for you and created you to be equal. Not more and not less!

Let's take another look at children. Children just are. They are just what they were created to be. They are living in their full being as an individual. Unless someone tells them otherwise, they are full-throttle equals. They don't see color or race. They don't see nationality or tribe. They don't see sect or religion. They don't see the difference. Now and again they may grab another child's toy, but that is just because they want it. It's not that they want it because they are superior and someone else is inferior. They just want it. They aren't stifled with labels or boxed in with limitations. Everything for them is a possibility.

Their imaginations are tremendous and wondrous. And their potential has no limits!

So never stop a child from living out their divine purpose. And as for you, take a tip from a kid. In fact, go play with some kids. Observe them and pay attention! Go back in time and become a kid again. You can do it. If there's one thing you will learn from this book, it is that you can do anything, right? Anything is possible. Everything is a possibility. And nothing is impossible. So get busy! Try and fly. Make it happen!

Make each minute count for something. When we are talking about equality, I believe one of the most important areas where we all feel we need our equal time - is with our thoughts and our feelings. I know for me, the quickest way to get me upset is for someone to interrupt me when I am talking or try to talk over me. It makes me feel they don't believe I matter or what I think matters. I feel disrespected, and I feel they think I am less important than they are. Or maybe they think I am stupid. What about you? Does this upset you too? It is important that we take ownership of our thoughts and feelings. Recognize we have the right to express them, in a respectful way, of course. We shouldn't go around shouting or disturbing others just so we can be heard and spew our opinions out on others. But we do have a right to our opinions, do we agree on that?

Well then, if we are being an equal person that means that others have the right to their opinions too. They are just doing what we are doing, owning them, right? Why is she asking me all these questions and making this so hard? Every time I think I am getting my way she comes up with something I must think about that makes me realize how hard it is to be equal, and not selfish. I know, change is hard - but it is exciting too! I bet you didn't know there was this much to think about. Let's make a game of it and pretend it is fun. Which one of our "E" words was that one? Was it endorphins? Or was it ______?

Where has all of this brought us so far? How about being enlightened to all the possibilities. How about enlightened to all the greatness and wonder in this world? And how about enlightened to all the excitement and beauty this planet has to offer? Okay, have I got you back now? Have I got you interested again? Good!

It's time to have a head-on collision. You will want to have this one – it won't hurt you, it will bring out the CEO in you.

Excuses

What are excuses anyway?

Again to the Merriam-Webster we go. Excuses: *"Justifications, reasons or explanations not necessarily true, given in order to make something appear more acceptable or less offensive." "False reasons that enable somebody to do something he or she wants to do or avoid something he or she does not want to do."*

What can we take away from these definitions? How about not necessarily true, offensive, avoid and inept which describes everyone negative and everyone uninspiring. Are you filled with excuses? Do you know someone or live with someone who is full of excuses? What are you going to do about it?

Think about this example from someone's life:

My high school teacher asked my reason for being late to class. I had dawdled on the way, so I made up something. She said, "That's not a reason, that's an excuse" 55 years later I still remember that, and the lesson I took from it.

-anonymous

Another: *Any excuse goes hand in hand with low self-esteem.*

-anonymous

What are your comments on these two insights into our world of excuses?

What pops into my mind is, *"To be or not to be".*

William Shakespeare

Ironically, this is the subtitle of this chapter. Excuses is one of those "not to be's". The ones we want to try to keep out of our life. So don't be full of them or "excuse"-full. Don't tell yourself it's alright to be second best and to settle for mediocre. Don't sabotage yourself with fear, procrastination or the "I'm not good enough's". No excuses that you can't realize your dream or change your life, because - "They won't like it, understand it or let me do it". It doesn't matter if no one likes your painting, writing, choice of clothing or the way you wear your hair. Who says "they" are right? Why do you need "their" approval?

Validate yourself! Your opinion matters. The excitement and rush, the passion you get from doing what you love and what you know you were meant to do - is the best medicine for what ails you.

Since you are supposed to, "not to be" full of excuses. What *are* you supposed "to be" full of? You are to be full of, **excusable**. That's right. Excusable is like excuses brother-in-law. Or, as in the case of my in-laws, outlaws.

Excusable, forgives. Excusable is a team player. Excusable gives everyone a break now and again. And that everyone includes you too! Give yourself a break. Excusable seeks the truth and realizes that sometimes you have to settle for reality. Striving and getting are two different words, and can be two different worlds. We must always strive to be the best and see the best in others, but acknowledge often times it is in the striving that the "best" comes out. Not necessarily, "the perfect" but we aren't looking for perfect.

Take a chance. Trust your voice, make no excuses. It's time that frog got changed into the prince or princess. That frog has been a frog for so long it has forgotten it's a CEO, right?

Stay on course. Use that voice, your inner compass that always points north to the truth of who you are, who you were meant to be. Try to do things for the sake of trying them, not for the goal of perfection or great success. Do it for the fun of it, for the glory of it, and for the purpose of it. And please allow disappointment, because disappointments will come and they will go. And remember that, *they will go*. They are part of life, and they will be a part of you. But only a small part, unless *you* make them the whole, the whole of who you are. And the easiest way to do that is not to try.

Every experience you have had since you were born has formed you into who *you* are today. Changing your life and making it what it was intended to be is: taking these experiences of who you are today, and matching it to who you were created to be. Think about that for a minute, then, go play the "Match Game".

Now I want you to do one more thing for me before we move on. I want you to go out and rent the movie, "Facing the Giants" and watch it. If you had to do a book report on it, or should I say, movie report, you would easily get an A+. There are so many lessons to be learned, opportunities to see past the obvious, focus on the obscure, and uncover priceless treasures that it would make Mark Twain jealous. So put this book down and go and do!

Seriously, I hope you do watch this movie. The affect it will have on you will be profound!

Next...?

Expectations

Expectations is just a word, but oh! What a word!

Do others seem to ask too much of you? Do you ask too

much of yourself? Maybe you're tired and are ready to stop the madness and free yourself. What are expectations anyway?

Merriam-Webster educated me to the fact that the first use of the word expectation was in 1540. Now, how the heck do they know that? Was Webster or Merriam around to hear it the first time? If not, how do they really know the first time it was used? Personally I think it was in 1492. You know, Columbus sailed the ocean blue in 1492. Now those were some expectations!

"Hey, Isabella!"

"Yes, Chris."

"Everyone's saying the world is flat, but I bet you all the gold it will cost to build three ships, that I can sail around the world and not fall off." "What do you say?" "Are you in?"

Or maybe it was even earlier than that. There's that story about the monk sitting at his writing desk when the head monk comes in and says, "Francis, hurry, I need ten copies of the Dead Sea Scrolls!"

Now that's pressure. Those are some really high expectations!

Isn't that how you think of expectations, as a negative, someone putting some unreasonable amount of pressure on you to do something impossible? Oh, by the way – do it quick! And, if you continue to look at it this way, then it's one of those "not-to-be's". But what if you change your perspective? What if you use your creative genius, clear your neuro-pathways, and change the path to a clear and concise one? Simply put, what if you learn the true meaning of the word?

Good old Merriam-Webster defines expectations: *"The anticipation of something happening, a confident belief or strong hope." "A notion of something, a mental image of something expected." "Prospects for future."* In this context our word, expectations, has great and uplifting synonyms - anticipation, hope and belief. Maybe the truth is expectations are something we need to have and hold on to. Just maybe, it is the expectation itself that is the key to the mystery of change, the need and the desire to change lives!

Expectation is not a wimpy word. It is not flimsy or frail. It is confident and strong. It provokes a mental image that stirs up powerful feelings and passion. Doesn't this sound like it is related to your ultimate purpose? When you are full of expectation or expectant you are on guard, you are looking for something special to happen. You are paying attention. You are mindful and alert. You are fully living, and not just a waking sleepwalker.

If you look for something good to happen you will find it. You will see it when it appears. Did you know that? Do you realize *that* is the difference between you getting what you want, and you wanting something and settling for what you get? Seek and you shall find. Look and you will see. Keep your eyes closed and you will miss everything. But how do you know when you have gotten *it* if you don't know what you are looking for or wanting?

Ah-hah! So not only do you need to live your life in a state of expectancy every day, you must recognize *it* when it arrives. You must confidently look forward to each and every day because today may be the day when *it* comes. And what is *it*? Good question! You are paying attention. *It* is different for everyone. *It* is connected to the passion that arises when you are doing something you truly love to do.

Imagine this, "Expectation is the fulfillment of the hope and belief there is more, much more". Not more money, more goodies or trinkets to accumulate, but the *more* of an actualized life. A life changed and a life full of change. And until that life does arrive. Until that day when *it,* your realized ultimate purpose, arrives, "knowing" and having the faith that it will arrive - *must be enough.* This again is where walking the day out along side your architect will increase your ability to make this happen.

So what am I asking you to do? I am asking you to always live in a state of wonder. I want you to live in a state of awe. Look around you! There is beauty everywhere and in everything. Visualize what you want, what you want your future to be. Visualize waking up each morning excited because you are living your dream – your ultimate purpose. Expect and respect. Expect the best for yourself. Expect the best in and for others. Respect the realization that if you are living in a state of expectancy, so must others. But what if your expectancy clashes or interferes with theirs?

Again, here's another *Ah-hah* moment. This is where sitting down and enjoying a nice, hot cup of tea would really help. I love the English. No matter what is happening, tragedy or elation, nothing interferes with their daily "spot of tea". They really know how to live.

What do you do if what you believe and hope for with every ounce of your being goes against what someone else believe and hopes for with all of their heart? This is where knowing your self and knowing others is so important. Because if you do, instead of unrealistic expectations ruining lives; *realistic goals will change lives*. Think about it.

I'd like to give you another little exercise to do. Again, this one will work on your imagery. A good friend of mine taught me this one:

Sit down in a comfortable chair, close your eyes and let your entire body relax. Think about yourself in all the areas of your life. As you are doing this, imagine what type of animal you are in each of those situations. Are you a tiger at work but a road-kill possum at home? Or maybe it's the other way around? You are mean as a snake at home but a pushover in the workplace. Or are you an efficient multi-tasker squirrel at work but a lazy walrus around the house? Really get into it! Take the time. This is important!

Once you have the two or three animals clearly in your mind see yourself holding them in your hands. Remember to keep your eyes closed, very important. Then I want you to smash them together. That right, clap your hands together hard and annihilate those babies!

Okay, now you can open your eyes. With all seriousness look and tell me what you see. Do you see pieces of animals lying everywhere? Do you think you could put those pieces together and make a new animal? Do it. Create your new animal. What is it?

Mine was a giraffe. It was the new animal I made out of the bits and pieces of my lion and new-born puppy, the animal I was at work and the animal I was at home.

Once you have your new animal standing in front of you, introduce yourself to it. This is the new you! This is the new balanced you. This is the *"you"* that will be able to handle situations in all areas without the highs and lows and without the passive-aggressive ups and downs.

The last thing you must do which is vital to your successful transformation is you must feed and nurture your new pet. It is not a caged animal to be locked up and forgotten about. You must pay attention to it. You need to take it for walks, remember to give it food and water. Take the time to pet and cuddle it.

I'll give you a hint of what I did for my new animal to make it real and plant it fully in my life. I would imagine my giraffe with a large pink bow around its neck nibbling at the tree tops. That's visual. That's hard to miss driving down the highway. I made it a point to work on my new animal daily. It became a friend of mine. I would see giraffes everywhere; in stores, in restaurants and in my dreams. Suddenly everywhere I looked I was surrounded by giraffes!

Do you know why my new animal was a giraffe? Giraffes are big but gentle and beautiful. Pretty good combination, don't you think? What is your animal and why do you think it is what your innermost self chose? You know that's where the choice came from, don't you?

Oh, by the way. Don't forget to journal this whole experience and all the differences you notice in every area of your life. Good luck! And good hunting.

And our next "E" changer is:

Emotion/Emotions

I believe this is where the intensity of our passion collides with everyone else and everything else. This is where we encounter what is lurking around the corner trying to dissuade us. And where we find out what lies down deep in our hearts, and every so often flies out and zings someone in the kisser. I guess it's time we made friends with our accuser, our rogue, our humanism. But before we do that, I have a question for you. Where have all our heroes gone?

There have always been good guys and bad guys, heroes and villains. They would fight each other but in the end, the hero always won. The hero out-witted the villain and made us feel safe. But now the villains have taken over, they are in charge and no one feels safe anymore. What's that all about? When did that happen? Did we forget to listen? Did we lend a blind eye and look the other way? Were we too busy or bored or just too complacent and lazy?

We need a revival! I vote for a good old-fashioned "good guy" revival – Superman revisited. We need a living, breathing, flesh and blood Zorro, Lone Ranger or Spidey. You ask, "What got your juices going this morning?" Well, I was watching the Today Show and Andrew Garfield was being interviewed. Do you know who he is? He is the new Spiderman, old pip, and he had some very interesting things to say. It seems that he really campaigned hard to get the role. And when he was asked why, his response was, "Because Spiderman is a hero and we need heroes in the world today."

That got me thinking. Not only was he right, but it was more than that. It is about how far we have strayed, how far we have fallen from true heroism out-smarting and outweighing the villains. Why do we want to hear the shockingly bad and not the shockingly good? Why are we not fighting harder for good role models for our children and young people? Is this another conspiracy? I'm big into conspiracies. Or is it so when the really bad stuff happens we won't be so shocked? Since we are already so shell-shocked?

I guess the good role models don't sell as many magazines or commercial ads on TV like the sex scandals, athletes on steroids, embezzled campaign funds and mistresses do. Pity, I'm glad I am old enough to remember "Bonanza" and "Leave it to Beaver" the *first time around.*

I wondered why I was so impassioned until I realized it

arrived right on time. It's all about emotion and emotions. Emotion is your gauge, your signal to let you know when you are low on oil, or running too hot. If you pay *mindful,* attention to your emotions and your feelings, you will know when something is wrong or when something is right. We are all intricately made and more highly tuned than a Ferrari. Our architect is a master technician and installed a motherboard in each of us, which is more delicate and more accurate than any computer could ever be.

So let's take a closer look at emotions. In fact, let's dissect them. The Free On-line Dictionary tells us that emotions are: *"Heightened feelings or disturbances in the normalcy of our body." "They are bodily feelings associated with mood, temperament, personality, disposition and motivation." "They can be affected by levels of hormones in our body." "They are spontaneous, not a conscious effort on our part."*

Since they are spontaneous, must they be uncontrollable? And since they are usually physiological and behavioral changes are produced by them, it sounds to me like we are in for a bumpy ride! What do you think? Does this all sound complicated to you? Well, humans are complex little human beings. Incredibly made to withstand enormous amounts of stress and pain, yet step the wrong way coming down the stairs and you could end up with your leg in a cast. We cry at weddings and the birth of babies, yet we can shoot someone with a gun, or run someone over with a car out of pure anger. Sweet and sour, tough and delicate, brilliant and ignorant = us humans.

Emotions: fear, love, hate, envy, jealousy, happy and sad. Since they are an automatic response system in your body, it is out of the total of your life experiences that your emotions emanate. Security and love during childhood should produce generous, loving adults; whereas, rejection and insecurity during childhood often produce fears and negative behaviors.

But physical ailments, pain, and varying levels of hormones can also produce all sorts of emotions too. That is why emotions are accurate forecasters and great barometers of what is really going on inside you. Since they spill out before you can hold them back, they are the overflow of what you have most. Or at least what you have most at that time. No one is perfect, so love won't be oozing out of you all the time. But, hopefully hate won't be shooting out all the time of you either.

So, since this chapter is about the "to be's" and the "not to be's", how do emotions fit in? Well obviously, you want to be or want to have the good emotions and not the bad ones, right?

A lot easier said than done. Because if your emotions are automatic, how can you control them? Let's take a look back at what we have already learned. Since emotions overflow from what is inside and should a negative emotion explode through, it must be signaling that something is wrong. You have not dealt with an issue, forgiven someone, or forgiven yourself.

Maybe you are holding on to and harboring something negative in your life, or a combination of the above. It can be something else too. You could be overworked or in pain. Maybe working a job you hate and taking it out on everyone around you. Could you be holding in anger and feeling resentful, not being transparent by speaking up and voicing those resentments? What else comes to your mind?

What do you do? Do you just ignore it? Keep doing what you have been doing and ending up with the same result? That's the definition of insanity you know. We've already talked about that one. The answer is "No"! You must do the work to rid yourself of this dead weight, this old baggage. So the emotions you are feeling are the "to be's" not the "not to be's".

Go back and look at what we talked about in the beginning of this book. The words examine and excavate will help you identify and work through the process of getting free. Another important step is to clarify what you are really feeling. Find out what that emotion is really telling you about yourself and your body. What is it really representing? A high feeling of anger can really be embarrassment, inadequacy or the fear of something. It can also be a way of getting rid of someone in your life before they "dump you". That's the fear of rejection.

So you see... what you see or "hear" is not always what you get (what really is). You are a complicated little "critter" and it takes a lot of effort to know yourself and to understand others. I suggest you check out the Internet, really the quickest way to find an "emotions" checklist, and then test yourself. Think about the people, places and things in your life and feel the emotions that rise up in you with each one. Is it appropriate? Is it telling you something is wrong? Has it uncovered something you have been trying hard to keep hidden? Keep digging, you'll find your treasure.

Let's take a few minutes and do a little review of these first three nouns:

Excuses **Expectations** **Emotion/Emotions**

Can you see how these three fit together? Which ones are your most troublesome areas? Each one has a healthy and an unhealthy side. How can you move yourself from the unhealthy side to the healthy side? How much are you willing to invest? Aren't you worth investing in? Study the following:

<u>Healthy</u> – No excuses - only truth

No unrealistic expectations on others or yourself

+ Reachable ones - on course with your ultimate purpose

No issue stuffing - it produces explosive negative emotion

Instead: try using your emotions as a *"range finder."*

= Equals a clear path to your ultimate life's purpose!

<u>Unhealthy</u> – Procrastination and the "blame game"

Resentments and guilt

+ Sick relationships, situations, bad choices

= Equals chaos and a disaster of major proportion!

Which one will you choose? Which one have you already chosen? Which one have you let happen to you? If the answer is not the one you want for your life, what are you going to do about it?

Your answer will lead you square into our next life-changing "E" word:

Email

"Oh come on. How can email have anything to do with changing my life?"

You may think it curious I chose this word since quite often I rank on the "computer age" and reminisce about the "good ole days" before megabytes. But let me explain. I intentionally chose email because *everyone understands what it is!*

If I would have chosen excommunication you might be scratching your head and thinking I have lost my mind, gone too far. But alas, I have not gotten off the elevator on the wrong floor or walked into the men's room instead of the ladies room, at least not today. You see, communication is an art and email is *not.* Communication requires an encounter, email does *not.* Communication requires skill, email does not. Now you know the reason behind my comparison of email to excommunication.

To me it's like we have taken a step back and become introverted, like a turtle retreating into its shell, or a snail taking refuge in its escargot. We are hiding behind our computers, cell phones and other gadgets, eyes diverted downward. Never reaching the pair of eyes we are communicating with on the other end; beautiful eyes, inquisitive eyes, and most importantly – expressive eyes. We are missing half of the story by just getting a "short-hand" version of some message, my BBF. See (with your eyes) what I mean?

Did you know if you look up email on the internet there are pages and pages of information about it? So many pages, so many details, too many details! There's only one I singled out and that is **@.** @ = at, and it means I have to spend too much time @ my computer checking my emails, most of which I end up deleting anyway because they are junk mail. The time I waste doing this I could have had a wonderful face-to-face encounter with someone, heard the tone in their voice, seen the reaction in their face and made a lasting memory. You remember what a memory is: an encapsulated caption of time and space with another human being expressed in a way that can't be compared to an "electronic blurb". I guess you know where I stand on this subject. Ha, ha, ha...

As a society, we have forgotten how to communicate with ourselves. We have also forgotten how to communicate with our architect. I don't mean "Hey, how ya doing, have a nice day". I mean a constant and continuous open line of communication. That steady stream of LISTENING and then bouncing your thoughts and ideas back. What's your architects' opinion? Sound silly? Definitely not! It is not only logical but imperative for a purposefully changed life. That life you want, your life, on the direct path to your ultimate purpose. You don't have to physically *see or hear* someone to know they exist and have meaning in your life. Think about the times you have had to decide to do, or not to do, to say, or not to say something potentially groundbreaking in your life. Haven't you run this thought through your head, "What would mom or dad or so-n-so do? What would they think?" Then you felt you just *knew* the answer? Well, it's the same with your architect, the creator of you. How can you be on target with your purpose, if you are out of sync with him? Think about it.

And as far as the idea of continuous communication with yourself, you better be doing this one. How else will you be sensitive to your needs, fears, hopes, dreams and passion? You have to know *you* better than you know anyone else in your life. Your future, *your life-changing future* depends on it.

"How do I do it?" you ask. Me? I talk to myself, but that's a whole other story.

You have to be totally honest with yourself. Honest about what you want and don't want, how you are feeling right now, what needs to change and what needs to stay the same. Think about what really makes you excited, passionate and happy. You have to listen to your heart, your soul, your inner light. It is always trying to lead you, that inner light. But you get so distracted and busy with everything going on around you, you miss it. You must be quiet, listen - just *be.* You don't have to be doing something or saying something all the time. You could be using that as a crutch so you don't really look at yourself and deal with what needs to be dealt with.

If I don't get quiet time, I am mean, like a bear. I get stressed, anxious and unhappy. I need some time with nature or doing something creative. Eating an ice cream cone or driving in my car with the music playing loud is great for letting that part of my brain, (the part that isn't concentrating on driving), be free long enough for brainstorming. Letting ideas flow, breaking through and getting answers to questions I have been wondering about. Quiet time is important and essential for gaining insights into yourself and others. *Get clarity!* Let that longing inside you for a deeper understanding and a deeper connection to your innermost self take over for a while. You can do this!

You are a problem-solver. Ignore the lies you have been telling yourself for years. Construct a whole new life; a life that brings you satisfaction, pleasure, and a sense of well-being. A life that offers you a connectedness to a cause and the source that is greater than you are. See how you fit into the big scheme of the universe. Bring your little 2 x 2 piece of the puzzle to the 1,000,000 piece mega-puzzle cover-all, and see what you discover. Make your puzzle piece glorious, rich in color and depth, bright and shiny. Make it an intricate part of the bigger puzzle picture. Realize that without your piece of the puzzle, the puzzle is incomplete. It can't be finished. *You are instrumental to its perfection!* You! You are! Don't look around like I am talking to someone else. You know I am talking to you.

Embrace the truth and wear it! It is your badge of honor. It is honorable to play an important part in this universe. It also is a privilege. This is where many people say, "Whoa, it's beginning to get too heavy for me, I travel light". Well, hate to break your bubble kid, but there is a responsibility of being a fellow human. You weren't birthed a pup or a fawn. You weren't created as a little fluffy bunny. You were born a higher being, one with caretaking stamped on your forehead. That means taking care of yourself and taking care of others who you meet along your journey as part of your ultimate purpose.

Don't forget to pay attention to your non-verbals. How are you walking? Are you walking down-trodden or with a spring in your step? Your eyes wide-open, eagerly seeking out what life has to offer. Do you constantly sigh and talk about what's wrong with your life? Or do you smile and find the positive in every situation? How about stress-related ailments? Do you suffer with headaches, backaches, nervousness, a lack of concentration or the inability to enjoy? Pay attention everyday to what your body is trying to communicate to you. And since you are human, and all the other people in the world are human too, you must notice. Look for the non-verbals in others. Pay attention to what they say and then what they do. Do they match? What are their non-verbals signaling to you?

It's like behavior modification meets "the most wonderful life you have ever dreamed of, ever!" Talk to yourself! Find out what is burning inside you. Change! Make it happen!

How do you know who you can be if you don't try? You must look past the fear. Take a chance! Make history, make *your* history. Make a history that will affect others; your family, your sphere of influence, your world.

You have someone inside waiting to be set free. Who knows who it could be? Nelson Mandela was just a person before he freed the person inside and changed a nation. Who knows, you could be a mother or a father of a future Mandela. *You* could be a future Mandela! You could be another Gandhi, or Mother Teresa or JFK!

Or maybe it's the courageous man from Bussey, Iowa featured on the Today Show this morning. Is he famous? He is to the residents of that small town of less than 500 residents. But what a town!

This man was in a devastating car accident that should have killed him. He was told he would never walk again. But he did, with the help of his town. The town helped to raise his son, he was a single dad. When his son grew up the town raised the money to send him to college. The man wanted to give back for everything that he and his son had been blessed with. He tried to join the National Guard, but because he had broken his neck in the accident, they turned him down. He had so much hardware, so many plates and screws implanted in his body that he was practically a toolbox all by himself!

So you know what he did? He taught himself how to paint, beautifully I might add. And for the last ten months has painted an outdoor mural on the side of one of the downtown buildings. He has painted his town and its people living out their daily lives, to give something very personal back to them for all they have done for him and his son. To show the gratitude he has down deep in his heart. Wow! He lives with physical pain everyday, and with this project his pain has increased dramatically. But his response to this was, "The more the pain, the more the beauty. And that is what I see everyday, beauty."

Makes you feel ashamed when you complain of a little headache, doesn't it?

Don't waste what you have. Make the most of what you've got. Be an inspiration. Change a life, yours first and then someone else's. One person *can* make a difference! This is what saying "no" to the email and saying "yes" to communicative encounters means. You are a communicator. Put that on your resume! You are an expert in communication, whether you do it well or you stink at it. You are still one. Not communicating is still communicating, it just moves to the non-verbal side of the field. Be a watcher of people. Make a game of it.

Communicating is like playing football. The quarterback better be on the same wave length with the wide receiver. Or when that ball sails fifty yards through the air towards the end-zone, it's going to hit someone in the head, break his nose and the team loses the game. Game over. Communicating always involves at least two, the sender and the receiver. Otherwise a tree will fall in an unoccupied forest and not make a sound, no one to hear it. It has no ones' eardrums to bounce off of.

So add expressive being and expert communicator to your "to be" bucket, and drop "email" into the "not to be" bucket. "Uh-oh, I hear the silence and can sense your aura of being overwhelmed in the air." Even though it's better than being underwhelmed, it is not advantageous to you. Your stress level rises, the desire to give up and shut down takes over, and it defeats the whole purpose in having this dialogue. See that? This is a perfect example of an expressive communication and being sensitive to others feelings – in real time. So what am I going to do about it?

What is my answer to you? Another "E" word:

End-zone

"Great!" you say. How can more work help make me less overwhelmed?"

It will, if it accomplishes what I hope it will. Let's give it a try. Do you feel evicted from your life? I mean your old life? I hope so!

The victory is in the running not in the winning. Merely by running we are moving towards our purpose. But you must take that first step, that giant leap. Your destiny starts with one single step. It's not whether you win or lose; it is how you played the game. Winning isn't everything. It's just a thing. It's not about finishing or finishing first. It's all about the running. Sound familiar? Have you heard these before? Did they mean anything to you, or did you blow them off like so many of us do?

It's like the marathon runner who in the late stage of the race tore his Achilles tendon. It looked like he would not be able to finish the race. But in his heart the goal he dreamed of for so long was to complete a marathon. Now it looked like that dream was dead. Then pushing his way out of the crowd was the runners' father. He put his son's arm around his neck, shouldered the burden, and slowly, but with great pride, helped his son over the finish line. It didn't matter they came in last. It didn't matter that the time was late as they crossed that finish line. They had made it to the end-zone! The son had believed and realize his dream. Stay the course and search for something more. It's the "something more" that gets us out of bed in the morning to face another day with all its challenges and opportunities. It's the "something more" that puts the twinkle in our eye and the fire in our belly.

There comes a time in each of our lives when we must do what we were meant to do. If we don't, there's a part of us that withers, sours and dies. That sour withered part becomes the regrets and the resentments of life. They fester and become the jealousy and envy of life. *They harden and become the end of life, before death.*

It's all about running the race, *your* race. No one else's race, yours alone...

I know I mentioned the horse Secretariat before and her owner Penny Chenery. I've watched that movie, Secretariat" endless times and each some nuance glares out at me, and makes me realize how powerful this story is. Penny had put her own personal desires on hold, as many women did back in the 50's and 60's. But when her mother died, she had to step up to the plate, not only to make sure her dad was taken care of but to see that his life's work – his legacy, would not die. Her dad tells her to run her race. Her dad tells her to let the red horse, Big Red, "Secretariat" - run his race. She has so much on her mind *she hears what he says but does not really listen to what he is saying.*

To make a long story short, after years of juggling two households, bringing the horse farm out of the red, and developing just about the most famous race horse that ever lived, she finally gets it. By doing all that, she did finally run her race. She had realized her purpose for herself and for her family. Now she was about to do the last thing she had to do. She had to let go, and let the horse run *his* race. Not her race. Not for the farm, the family, or for anything or anyone. It was for that horse's purpose. He was about to do something impossible, something that had never been done before. And to do that, he had to be *allowed* to run *his* race. He had to be given permission by the most important person in his life, and he had to decide "yes" it's time. It's my time. He had his own ultimate purpose to live out.

Yes, every living creature has their own ultimate purpose.

But let's concentrate on you – we are talking about your ultimate purpose. Your purpose is more than authentic. It is empowered energy. It is you in your entirety, the sum of all your parts. It is what emanates from you. It oozes out of every pore of your body. Your essence is the *you*, you have spent a lifetime perfecting. Perfecting until it is so natural and so much who you are, you don't have to "try" to be it. It is you! You are it! You breathe it out of your toenails, and drink it through your hair. You can smell it through your earlobes and taste it through your elbows. Take a whiff! Take a taste. Your essence is the most powerful thing you possess. It's the most powerful thing about you. It can change a life, a town, a world. It precedes you and it stays long after you are gone.

Have you ever been around someone that even before they enter a room there is an aura of anticipation, a spark of electricity so strong that once they walk through the door the whole room lights up? Their essence calms a storm, insights laughter from fear, makes time fly by, and makes you smile. Everyone wants to be around them. They don't even really know why except they just feel better when that person is there. And even after they leave, that essence lingers on like a warm blanket and a cup of hot cocoa. You never want to leave their presence, you want to get all snuggle"ly" in it.

Do you want to really feel good? Stand up for something or someone. That's it! Take a stand! Put something you value on the line for another person, a cause, or something helpless. Feel the rush! Automatically your body holds your head up higher. Your step is more assured and your thoughts are clearer. I don't know if it's a rush of adrenaline, dopamine, or serotonin, or what, but it's a "Dudley Do-right" manifestation. It's more than a natural high. It's a natural "higher" use of your brain and flesh body suit. You just aren't hanging around waiting for something to happen, for someone to do something. *You* are the *one* the others have been waiting for! So what are you waiting for? Do it! *Just do it!*

Intermission

I mean it is time for an intermission. I am assuming you have already been putting into practice what we have been talking about all this time. If you have, then you have already noticed many changes in yourself and in your life. This is the point when you need to reflect on them and grade your progress. What has changed? Are you feeling more power and peace in your life? Do you feel a connection with your architect? Do you want more of it? Has your confidence level risen and your CEO, The Chief Executive Officer, of your life emerged?

No matter how good your answer is to these questions, celebrate it. Celebrate your willingness to recognize you want more. Pat yourself on the back that you no longer want to open your eyes in the morning and say, "Is this all there is?" "Is that all there is, really?"

You have taken steps to know more, do more and have more life! You have realized you do have a purpose and you want to live it! So party! Party hardy, Marty!

Zzzzzzzzz...

I've been getting a few "z's" while you have been gone. Are you refreshed, bright-eyed, bushy-tailed and raring to go? Good. Me too!

Next very important "E" word to explore:

Excellence Extraordinary Exceptional Elegant Elated Euphoria

Whoa, that's a whole bunch of "E" words, not just one. Which one are we talking about? Take your pick!

Which one do *you* want?

Why not choose them all? I know *I* want to be all of them.

Whichever one you choose will represent the entire group, all for one. Wouldn't you want your friends to tell others that you *are* extraordinary, exceptional and you stand for excellence? Wouldn't you want to feel elated and full of euphoria about your life? And who wouldn't want to be and feel elegant? We want it all!

How do you have it all?

Live a life of excellence. Whatever you do - do it with all your heart, mind and soul. Do it boldly and give it 110% of your attention, time and resources. Be extraordinary – **extra-**ordinary. I don't know about you, but being amazing and astonishing is okay with me. I want someone to say about me, "She led an exceptional life. She did exceptional things. She lived her life in an incomparable way – more than anyone ever expected."

As far as elation and euphoria goes; joy, exhilaration, excitement, bliss, jubilation, and delight aren't too shabby of words if they were to describe how you felt about your daily life, are they? *It's a thrill to be alive!* This should be your daily mantra. This should be your banner. It should be what is invisibly stamped across your forehead. What others can't actually see, but they feel it pouring out of every particle of your being. They want to embrace it and embody it. They want to because it makes them feel so good just being in your presence.

Did all of that go to your head? Are you puffed up? Or bummed out?

Is the glass half empty or half full?

Look, I know no one is "Little Miss Sunshine" twenty-four seven but I am going to tell you a little secret. My secret is that: *"The secret lies in the belief,* not necessarily the outcome, *which will rise you up above whatever you believe your reality to be."*

Integrate and assimilate that one! It hinges on the philosophical, don't you think? It's much better than a fortune cookie. It's closing in on Confucius. But it really is true. Attitude or attitudes will make or break us. And we must start with ourselves. If you want an elegant, excellent and exceptional life, you are the only one who can make it happen or not happen. If you need to repeat that over again, please do. Say it until you believe it!

You want examples, ideas? How about some more questions...

Do you talk and treat your family like they were guests? You know what I mean. With guest, elegant guests, we put flowers on the table and bring out the good dishes. With family we say, "Come and get it" and expect them to get if off the stove themselves. With guests we take a bath, put on clean clothes, comb our hair and put on cologne. With family we walk around in our pajamas all day long, forget to shower, have dust balls in our hair and are odorous (not in a good way). What would happen if you took the time and made the effort to treat your *family* how *you* want to be treated? They might surprise you. They might rise to the occasion and soon you are humming a tune and smiling. You can't exactly remember why, but it sure does feel amazing!

Oh, so you live alone? Good! Then you need to be *exceptionally* good to yourself. Have fresh flowers on your table everyday. Look up a fancy complicated recipe and make it for yourself. Bring out the china, the wine glass, all the extra silverware (the little forks, spoons and knives), use a linen table cloth, napkin and toast yourself. **"You are extraordinary!"**

No excuses!

If you want it, go get it!

It's all in your mind any way, remember? You are what you believe. You are what you think you are. You have, and don't have, what you believe you have or don't have. You are your thoughts and beliefs. Not someone else's. Unless you absorb what they are saying about you, and then it is still what you believe.

And if you are waiting for someone else to make you happy or make you feel elegant, exceptional, or fill you with ecstasy and euphoria, you may be dead before it happens. You'll be pushing up daisies and wondering what happened. The trick is to do it first *then* others will do it too. In fact, until you do it, *others won't!*

If you don't value yourself others won't either. If you respect yourself so will others. And this goes for everything. Remember whether we like it or not, we are examples, others are watching us. They want to see what we do. We are leaders even by default. Are you a good one or a poor one? If you treat everyone the same and treat them well, others will follow your example. But if you treat yourself and others poorly, you have just given others permission to do the same. Remember, it's what you do and say when you think no one is watching that counts!

"Life astonishing!" Don't you want that printed after your name on your business card and your tombstone? Make your life count! Do you want people to say when you leave a room, "Thank God" or "Bring that person back – I want more!"

How about *you?* Do you want to spend time with you? Do you astonish and amaze yourself? If *you* don't even want to spend time with you, why should anyone else? You got some work to do baby! Get busy! But remember to relax and have some fun doing it. Otherwise it becomes a drudge and a chore. It becomes a boring duty. If that happens we start to hate it and instead of changing for the good, we have just increased the stuff we didn't like about our life in the first place. Hah!

So get busy self-generating the part of you that wants to regenerate, renew and restore. Ignore the part that is stuck or stuck in the mud, and concentrate on that part that has bought into the idea of change. The part that has shown up dressed in their work clothes ready to do some serious renovating. Hard hat in place, geared up to do some smashing and tearing down of old decayed walls, and loaded down with all new materials to build that stupendous skyscraper of a life. Is your sledge hammer and bulldozer ready? Motivated yet? What else do I need to do?

Something I am reminded to remind *you* of. Your life is not all about you. Can you accept that? Do you believe that? Are you willing to embrace that? This new stupendous skyscraper of a life is not just so you can sit around looking in the mirror admiring yourself. It is not just for you to hang plaques and accolades on the wall celebrating how wonderful you are. You may be wonderful and that's great. But hey, share the greatness!

Share your greatness but in the most humble of ways. The easiest way to lose your credibility and the respect from others is to tell others how great you are. If you have to tell someone about your own greatness than honey, *you ain't so great!* Your life is meant to be lived in such a way that you are great without knowing it, or trying to be it. In fact, some of the greatest people actually tried not to be so great. They were there to develop the greatness in others. That's what makes a great person. A great life lived with purity of passion and purpose. That is what we all need to aspire to do and to be. The more you make others look and feel good, the more your inner light shines and your soul is lifted up. Lifted up where?

The answer is, lifted up above the mundane and the humdrums of life, the day-to-day duties.

You need to live from your heart, mind, and soul. Live on a higher plane. That plane exists solely to encourage and empower, to bring comfort, and to put the needs of others above yours. And since we are all connected and all one anyway, what you do for others, you do for yourself. You don't have to be afraid to forget about yourself and boldly give your "all" for the betterment of this planet. Your architect designed this planet. So no matter how much you do and give, you can never give away more than your architect will replenish. You can't out-do him. Keep your mind open to what that replenishment is and what it might look like. Or else you might miss it!

> *You have been thinking about a cold glass of milk to drink and along moseys a cow. You are sitting on your front porch and this brown and white cow slowly walks across your yard, right in front of you. All you can say is, "I wish that cow would get the heck out of the way. I don't want to miss the dairy truck that is going to bring me my glass of milk."*

Get the point?

Live large! Live with gusto! And live as if today was your last. Guess what? It may be. Tell people you love them, give them a smile not a scowl, be patient, be kind and generous. Be there! Be active in body, in your thoughts, and in your time. Be 100% there, not always thinking of something or someone else. Worried about the next thing you have to do. Being in a hurry because you might miss an appointment you think is *so* important. Instead, if you live your life in such a way that you stay connected with your architect and source of your purpose, you will be exactly where you need to be precisely at the time you are supposed to be there. It’s in the plan. It is the plan. Go with it! Don’t try to figure everything out to the smallest detail. Keep your life open to the possibilities, nuances and the quirks of life. It is quite often in these quirks, the things you can’t explain, those unexpected encounters and the freedom in living inspired that will bring you what you have been searching for.

Are you journaling? Are you reminding yourself everyday how far you’ve come? How much progress you have made? Do it! This is your story, this is your life. Not only do you need to celebrate it, you need to remember it. Then you will be ready to share it. And if no one has told you lately, “I am proud of you”.

And, “I believe in you.”

It is not easy to look honestly at yourself and choose not to be afraid to change. So take a minute and pat yourself on the back. You deserve it! This morning I was sitting on my back porch having my wake-me-up-for-the-day cup of coffee, and I had a thought about hummingbirds. The thought was that hummingbirds and humans are very much alike. How so? First let me tell you a few things I have observed about birds in general.

Hanging from our back deck overlooking the park are

several birdfeeders. We have two for wild birds, two for finches, and two for hummingbirds. Now the wild birds are willing to cooperate and let other birds hang around and eat from the opposite side of the feeder. And if they are especially hungry, and if the feeders are empty, they will fly over to the window sill, chirp and even peck at the window to say, “Hey, where’s the grub?” They are assertive and ask for what they want.

Now the finches are interesting to watch also. Up to four or five finches will hang onto the bag of thistle eating away not minding the other birds. In fact, it is almost like they were saying, “Come and get it!” “Hey come on. Let’s see how many birds we can fit on this thing.”

Then here come the hummingbirds. On this particular morning I was wearing a super-bright pink duster and a few birds attacked me. They actually wanted to get nectar from me, thinking I was a flower and just so *darned sweet!* But then as I observed them I saw something very different.

First, they are very territorial. If there are two or more hummingbirds around you won’t see them eating together, sharing the love. Almost as soon as one sticks his little beak in and begins to extract the sweetness, here comes another hummingbird, dive bombs him and scares him away. It’s almost like a battle or a war is going on between them.

Secondly, you hear them coming and going. They flap those little wings so fast that it makes a loud “humming” sound, like about five bumble bees are flying overhead. And they fly so fast from here to there and back again. Their little hearts beating so fast and that adrenaline pumping. Either they make a sweet score or they have expended a lot of time and energy for nothing – just zooming and making a lot of noise.

Sounds a lot like us doesn't it? Maybe they are some sort of kin to us in a weird cosmic-naturalistic way. Let's see, selfish, not wanting to share, noisy, wasting time competing, not cooperating and "doing" but not accomplishing.

Hmmm...? Or is that hum? Sound like anyone you know?

The morale of this story...? Be a finch not a hummingbird.

Breathe...

"So now that I have breathed. What is the next "E" word that will change my life?"

And lucky number 19 is:

Endowed

To truly be all that you can be, you must be equipped and capable to carry out the necessary tasks to run your race. That, my friends, means being endowed. Endowed is a pretty cool word. It is multi-faceted. On one hand it implies being gifted or somehow acquiring the gifts to be able to do that "something extraordinary". Alright! We already know we want to be extraordinary, so endowed seems to fit right in.

It also implies that you have been equipped or that someone has equipped you to do a specific thing, equipped you to be special in some way. Well, we know our architect has made intricate plans for everyone. His plans for you are to be successful. It is logical then he would equip you to fulfill your ultimate purpose. Could be you were born with the talents like many artists and musicians are. Or it could mean that people, circumstances and opportunities have made their way into your life so you can obtain the knowledge and skills to fit that definition of being equipped.

Lastly, endowed implies that you are capable, not just gifted or equipped. But one step further. Being capable means you have tested your talents, gifts and equipment to make sure they work. You worked out all the bugs and kinks. You have sharpened your senses and intuitions, and fine-tuned them. You can now keenly survey the situation or problem, design, and put into place a plan to be successful in any endeavor you are attempting to do.

You have just used what you already knew and what you have learned to define endowed for yourself. What do you think about that? Do you feel capable? Do you now believe you have special gifts and talents that will catapult you to new heights in your life? Are you feeling endowed? Were you feeling this way a month, or two, or three ago? What changed? What have you discovered about yourself? How about your life and the lives of others?

If you were asked to grade yourself on the "endowed" scale of 0-10 with 0 being a slug and 10 being Superman or Superwoman, where would you fit along the curve? Me? Well today I am about an 8, pretty good. About a week ago I was only a 6, there was a pity party going on and I was the only guest. I was able to snap out of it and decided I best walk out the life I really have and not try to be one of those martyrs who always seems to come to a miserable end. Now back to you. What number did you pick for yourself? Why did you pick that number? If it's on the low side, why is it? What's making it low? If it's on the higher side, great! Why are you rating yourself so high today?

It's a great day for gratitude. In fact, everyday is a great day for gratitude.

Gratitude means we are thinking, not just walking in a stupor like a bunch of sheep to the slaughter. We have a firm grip on reality, and are able to evaluate and self-evaluate appropriately. Again, pat yourself on the back!

So let's look closer at endowed. Endowed is prosperity from within. It must start there. It must start from within and spread throughout and outward until it encompasses you in your entirety. It's not a spot of this here and a spot of that there. It is intentional and precise. It enlightens you to a point where you can transcend what you have done before, transcend the place where you have been to discover the new place where all things are possible.

It's the place where faith truly defines you. It where what you *can't see* doesn't matter because you believe. And your belief in yourself is greater than any other belief you may have. You sense it. That is how you *know*. And it is this *knowing* that is real and your truth. Pretty heavy, huh? Heavy is what us baby-boomers used to say when something was really profound, radically philosophical and mind blowing. Mind blowing and radically, again those 70's words. Memories...

If you want prosperity on the outside of your world, you must first have it on the inside of *you.* That's the principle again, sowing prosperity on the inside to reap prosperity on the outside. And what is key to that inside prosperity? You guessed it – being endowed. Here is the challenge. Is being endowed something you had nothing to do with, as in being born with it? Or is it something you can obtain or attain? If you asked ten people you might get a variety of opinions and a 50/50 consensus to that question. In truth, it doesn't matter. However you were able to arrive at the endowment and the prosperity within is your achievement. It's your triumph over the "almost's" and the "so close's" of the world.

Sometimes I think it just comes from time. The longer you are on this planet the more time you have to overcome the mistakes you have made, and see the mistakes of others unfold. The longer you hang in, the more opportunities you have to take a chance, and use your ever-changing ideas and ideals to perfect your craft of thinking. And thinking is a craft you know. It's a craft especially if you don't want to end up in jail or living on the street. So let's say I believe being endowed is more of a learned thing rather than a "gene" thing. The next step is to believe that you can be educated or educate yourself to be endowed, and equipped with whatever is necessary to successfully achieve your divine and ultimate purpose. You have to believe that when you reach your ultimate purpose you will have been endowed with exactly what you needed to fulfill it. It will be there!

Yes, that is exactly what I believe. I believe it so fully that I have written this book as your starting point to a changed life. It's your "Go" square on the Monopoly board and your starting block to the race that will take a lifetime to run. So run with the wind at your back, a cloud now and again to block the sun, and "manna" fresh everyday. Run...

Take a look at these next statements:

Whether you climb up the ladder of Success,
Or you slide down the ladder of Success,
Either will Change your life, forever!

Six Levels of Change

1. **Take action**
2. **Defining the difference – redefine yourself**
3. **Name it – claim it – words to live by**
4. **Apply it**
5. **Practice it**

   Your Ultimate Goal:

6. **YOU - let "it be" who you are**

Everything you have experienced in your life has added up and is the sum of the person you are today. And that is the total sum, not just some (as in part) I am talking about. It's the total of who you are, not just a little bit of who you are. Each experience you have is crucial to who you are today and who you will be tomorrow. What will make the difference? It is *what you do with each experience!* An experience may happen to you without your control, but you ultimately control what happens next. **You** have the control. It is you who has the power over the final outcome of that experience. Because you are the CEO, right?

All that we have been talking about so far points to this truth. You always have the power to be powerful or powerless, in your physical space or in your mental capacity. Another way to put this is: you can be free or you can be in prison - in body or spirit and mind. Your choice, you choose. Do you see bars?

As an adult no matter what our life circumstances we can make changes. Some may be big, some may be small, but *we must* take the *responsibility* of who we are. Not blame someone else for what we are not or what we have not. Is that some tough stuff for you to swallow? Good!

Experience

Let's define experience and then let's discuss, The Six Levels of Change. BING defines experience: *"An involvement in, or exposure to something over time." "Knowledge acquired through senses not through abstract reasoning." "Something that happens to some body, or an event they are involved in."* Some synonyms for experience are: understanding, capability, occurrence and encounter.

Personally, I choose encounter because it implies "it takes two." The "two" meaning: there is something or someone on the sending end and something or someone on the receiving end. It's a noun with action undertones. My kind of word! And if I may remind you again, you are what you think, you are what you *believe.*

When we talk about, The Six Levels of Change you will see that like the statements preceding it, you can either start at the top and go down or start at the bottom and go up. Either way, you will get the same results. Start at the bottom and you will see that **Take Action** needs to be the broadest piece, your foundational block. It's the first rung as you build and go up the ladder. And if you remember, this is where we talked about our first verbs: engage, excavate, embrace, examine, excuses and eecckk!. Next comes; **Define Yourself – Defining the Difference** which includes our discussions on envision, expand and equal. The third rung is: **Name it – Claim it.** Excellence and extraordinary, endowed and empower/empowered are the cornerstone for achieving this level. Number four and number five: **Apply it** and **Practice It** go hand-in-hand and may seem simple, but don't be fooled. They take work, and a lot of it. The discussions we've already had on exhale, endorphins, encourage, expectations, email and emotions will help you do the homework to succeed. And at the tippy-top is the goal, the prize. The hope is that you: **Let it be who you are – YOU!** And that *you* encompass what experience and end-zone gives us. But remember we are not done yet. We still have the last category of our "E" words, the last chapter and the final act of our play. We still need more to reach the top.

Is it all coming together for you? Are you finding a rhythm in it, your rhythm? I hope so. Let's talk a few more minutes. Let's talk about two words: entrepreneur and exploration.

Wait! First a little ditty...

Life is an experience

To be experienced

Live *your* life as an experience

Experience all.

For *all*, is to be experienced

Live *your* life as being experienced

Experience ALL!

It’s one of those, “I’m a poet and I don’t know it,” *experiences*. Aha!

We must have humor. It’s not an “E” word, but without humor we’d be bored and asleep. And not only couldn’t we stand others, we wouldn’t be able to stand ourselves either. So smile. Make yourself laugh, your face won’t break. They say that you have fewer wrinkles if you smile and laugh. Now I don’t know who “they” are but if that’s true, then all you have to do is look at someone’s face, wrinkly or wrinkleless to know if they are an “Oscar the Grouch” or another “Steve Martin”.

Okay, my two words. Up to this point we have been on an exploration. We have been journeying on our road to discovery, actually a self-discovery. This is the point where you should be able to feel different, think different, and see things differently. In fact, you should even be able to anticipate what may be coming next on the pages. I know you have been working hard. My excitement is being on this exploration with you. Because I am still alive, I too, am still on my journey to be fully the “me”

I am supposed to be. The second word I felt was important to mention, is entrepreneur. This is what you are, or what you will become from all your life experiences. You can choose to be a successful entrepreneur or an unsuccessful entrepreneur. How do you know which one you will be?

Because, you are the entrepreneur of your life! You are who you are from everything in your life up to this point. But that's only half of it. The other half will be what you have done with it. Entrepreneurs are self-made. Not that you have made yourself in the beginning, that credit goes to your architect. But once your brain and body was developed enough to make decisions, hello, the choices were yours. *The responsibility was yours, the buck stopped with you!*

The good news is that since you are responsible, you can change. You can make the changes that need to be made. It's your choice! That's why you are reading this book searching for answers and the truth. The truth is you can have the desires of your heart - a heart pulsating to the beat of your ultimate purpose. My hope is as we talk you will be sparked on to make this happen in your life, and make your life the best life possible!

Mush on...

NOTES

LET IT BE YOU

The real question is: How do you know if you have achieved "being it" or "it being you?" Or at least the "it" that "you" are being now? Because it's not enough to want to be it, or not want to be it, or trying "to be" or "not to be" – *it is who you are now.*

But before we delve further into that maze of to's, be's, and it's - let's do a short review. We all absorb and process information differently so I wanted to present another dimension to your learning curve and finish up what we already started. It is the idea that we can also slide down that ladder not just climb up it. We can look from the perspective of # 6 through #1 not just from #1 to # 6.

You can start with **YOU** because you are you. You have been **Applying** and **Practicing** what you know to do up to this point. Since that is true, you have **Named** and **Claimed** already who you are. Now **IF** you take a good look at yourself, examine and don't like what you see, then it's time to **Redefine Yourself** and **Take Action**.

Most things in life are a two-edged sword. This is no exception. Accepting this will help you immensely navigate your life. Take a look at the following diagram.

Change Your Life!

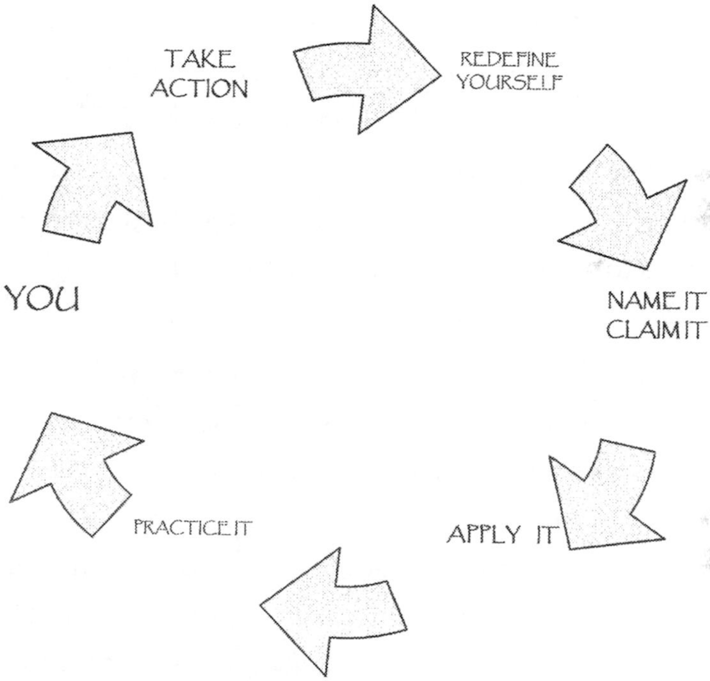

Change Your Life!

No matter if you are a lefty or a righty, an upper or a downer, or a backwards or frontwards person, you can utilize this game plan to change your life. It's up to you. Remember it's always up to you. You are the captain. Better yet, you are a consumer advocate and *you* are the consumer. You must be the #1 believer and promoter of yourself. If you don't believe in yourself and you don't advocate for yourself, why would anyone else? Why should anyone else?

You don't have to fly a plane and write your name across the sky, or buy expensive television commercials telling the world how great you are. If fact, if you do people will think you are obnoxious. All you have to do is walk, talk and act with authority, respect yourself. You have to make decisions which reflect that you value yourself, and then sharpen your "picker" so you make choices that are in your best interest, *and* the best interest of others. Remember, as part of those "good choices" you need to make are the universal principles of "what comes around goes around" and "we reap what we sow".

Take a moment and think back over the last week at all the decisions you made, and the ones you didn't make. And we know those you didn't make are still decisions in themselves. Did these decisions, these *choices,* reflect value and respect? Was your "picker" an advocate for you, the consumer? Or is your picker still broken? How well did you think through to the end of those decisions you were making, and was the outcome what you expected? It is critical for you to evaluate and re-evaluate progress every step of the way. It is something we all have to do, or we should be doing everyday of our lives, as we walk through this journey called life.

One last thing I want you to think about. What barriers were in your path that slowed you down or stopped your forward progress? More importantly - which barriers did you personally install into your life? What would have happened if you hadn't? Did you sabotage yourself? You do realize that putting those barriers in your way was self-defeating? You are defeating yourself! Why don't you want to succeed? Use several of those "E" verbs we talked about in the beginning to examine and excavate these hindrances in your life.

Take some time. There's no hurry, we can wait. This is too important to rush.

As I promised to reveal to you from the very beginning we are now ready for the final group of life changing "E" words. These words are descriptive. They describe the heart of "who you are", the adjectives. First "E" word in this category:

Energy

We are energy. You are energy. And as energy you are either emitting this energy purposefully, or having this energy emanating from you subconsciously. The result is - you are either building up your energy or exhausting and weakening your energy, and the energy around you.

Energy is power. It is a force, an influence. It is control and authority. Do you remember this from your science classes? Another thing they taught us about energy is that energy is eternal. It is perpetual, undying, everlasting, timeless and endless. Energy never disappears it just changes. If we have done our algebra, *we* are all eternal. You are eternal. You, as energy are eternal.

What else do we know about energy? Well, it can't be destroyed, it can take on various forms, and it can operate at low or high levels. But, it can't be contained or constrained under high pressure for long or it will explode. Does that sound a little bit like you? Let's take a closer look at these ideas and test their truth.

So as not to make this too technical like a textbook might be. Let's do this one notch below "too serious." Or as the *comic relief* part of me would say, "Not <u>toooo</u> serious!" In keeping with this spirit of fun, we are going to start with thirdly and move our way up to first.

<u>Thirdly</u>: *Energy can operate at low or high levels but it can't be contained or constrained under high pressure for long or it will explode*. Look back at the last month of your life. I am sure you have had days when you are full of get-up-and-go and feel like you can accomplish almost anything. You go to work, prepare meals, do chores, and chauffeur family members around. Maybe you even have time to unwind and spend with your significant other. Then there are others days when you can barely drag yourself out of bed and you want to drown the first person who asks you to do something for them. Your body feels like lead, your brain feels like cotton balls on steroids, and the last thing you want to do is look into the mirror. But you are still the same you. You are still the same amount of energy walking around in your flesh suit. You just don't "feel" the energy the same way everyday.

Why not? Could it be you have exhausted yourself yesterday

to the point where you do not have the will to be energized? Or maybe you have let someone else's negative attitude suck the life (energy) out of you. It feels like you have a fifty pound weight around your neck and all you want to do is hide in bed with the covers pulled up over your head.

Your energy didn't disappear. It's just at a low intensity. It's operating below your radar waiting for you to do what you need to do to replenish your eternalness. And then there are the explosions. Did you ever wonder why the day can be going perfectly glorious for you and BANG! One little thing; a remark, having to wait in line at the store, or getting cut off in traffic can raise your blood pressure, raise your voice, and sometimes raise your fists? What has been building up inside that has not been addressed? Why or what have *you* denied yourself clear visibility on? Your energy has been pressure-cooked, and now the steam is pouring out. Your lid is about to blow! *Look out!* Energy...

<u>Secondly</u>: *Energy can take on various forms.* Just like energy can be solid, liquid, and vapor/gas (i.e. ice, water and steam), so can the energy that forms you. Your body is made up of mostly water with some minerals thrown in to give you some substance. These minerals are the same ones found in; dirt mountains, rocks and trees. The only difference is the amounts and the combinations of those minerals and their properties. So as you age, and one day no longer have your physical body, those minerals return to nature and you literally are transformed. You take on a new form. Will you be a tree or a boulder? I don't know, but I do know you will continue to exist.

You will just exist in a different form. This means *all* of you - your physical presence, your eternal energy, your spirit.

And lastly, *First*: *Energy cannot be destroyed.* Think of energy as one big circle, like a band made out of precious metal, on your finger. It has no beginning and no end. It is strong. There are no weak spots in that solid band that can be broken. It is timeless and endless. It is everlasting and continuous. It was there since the beginning of time and will never cease. It is eternal; this energy, your energy, your spirit.

"To be" is to see all things through the eternal eye of energy and purpose. Your eternal energy makes your purpose possible. It is indestructible and will be here long after your body (your body of energy), changes form. It continues and will remain forever through the people you've touched, the changes you have brought about, and the differences you have made in this world. You are the circle. You are the band, and there are no weak spots in you.

Now, to be this eternal energy you must embrace this truth about yourself and understand that you remain long after you are gone "in the human sense of the word". You are part of all that was and all that will be. It is everything you are and everything you were meant to be, *this authentic you*. I know this is a big concept to absorb. But just let yourself soak it up a little while we look at the next "E" word which is:

Evolve

Evolve. Let that one slide over your teeth and tongue. Let it take its time as it slowly hits the surface and floats through the air. E-v-o-l-v-e. Evolve must be your middle name. You must give yourself permission, allow yourself to grow and change. It's okay. You must allow yourself to develop beyond who you are today. You cannot stay the same. You must never stay the same. Nothing stays the same. So you must always keep up with the "nothing" that never stays the same and the "everything" that is always changing. Move forward and advance. If you don't, you will be irrelevant to the world around you. It's important that you remain relevant to your family and friends. And you must remain relevant to your divine purpose, which eternally defines you.

You must continuously be open and accepting, using wisdom to discern the truth. Never be judgmental. Instead use all our "E" tools to make good decisions and choices which show respect to yourself and others. You must believe what is true, but understand the context in which you live and the effect your truth has on others. To evolve is to progress, to go forward without losing sight of your purpose and how your purpose heightens the passion and the purpose in others. As you allow yourself to evolve and become sensitive to others, you will be a welcomed addition to their life's purpose. And in no way will you diminish it. As an evolved entity you would never even dream of it!

Be like the butterfly; from caterpillar, to cocoon and pupae, to that beautiful-winged flutterer, flitting from flower to flower and back to earth again. As you become all that evolve is; you become the wrapping, the covering, the cocoon - for the change and progress that must happen. You become the envelope, the warm cloak that is a shield from the rain and the wind. You finally become one with the earth and your architect who fashioned you the way you are for your special purpose.

Every day you are different than the day before. You lose hair off your head and the old skin from your body. New hair and skin will replace the old (well for some, maybe not the hair). Your eyesight and hearing changes a fraction everyday. And thousands of cells die throughout your body, most of which will be replaced. On a daily basis, your memory, your hormone levels, your feelings, your weight, the color of your hair, and even your shoe size changes. Your physical person is changing and evolving so you better make sure the rest of you is keeping up! It is something you need to embrace. *Don't be afraid of it! It is who you are.* You need to become friends with it.

How will this ultimately help you? It will help you concentrate on what is important, and let go, (forgeeeet) of what isn't. Here's a simple example. You buy a new car. You love it. You wash it and wax it. You take it for rides to show it off. This excitement lasts for about a month. But then it's not new any longer. Now, you need to go back to what's important; your family, your friends, your job and the world. In a few years that wonderful car is going to start to fall apart, rust, need new parts, get dents, and you will get bored with it. If you have put all your time and energy into this inanimate object you will be: disappointed, lonely, penniless, and eventually without wheels.

Take a moment and let your eyes scan your surroundings. Think about what is now and what was before. Everything changes. Think about all of your relationships. Who was your best friend five years ago? Ten years ago? What did you think about the world back then? What do you think of the world now? What differences are there in your view of politics, movies you like, your favorite foods, and your hobbies? Have the changes come because you have evolved with the world, or have these changes come because you *did not* change?

Aha! That one should make you sit down and really take stock of your life. Try it. Do it! Remember, no fear. Be *fearless* in your search and discovery, your "rediscovery".

So, letting the nature of *evolve* define who you are means this: it will enable you to climb that ladder. That ladder to the level of understanding you have of the true importance of your life. Your life's purpose and how you affect others and the larger world around you.

And you thought the "E" words 1-20 were hard, huh?

These all encompassing, all-defining adjectives that describe who you are and who you must be, have great significance. They reveal the magnitude of the great gift you have been given: the gift of being a human with all your frailties.

Be fearless! Remember this journey is forever because energy never dies, right?

Be brave, be flexible and flex those muscles. Those brain muscles. You'd get a personal trainer for your body, right? So isn't this just as important? Maybe even a little more important? Use that brain, exercise it and feed it health food. It really can lift 1,000 pounds you know.

As I thought about this next word it occurred to me that it too, has two very distinctive parts, two distinct halves of its whole. There is a seriousness that is empowering, and there is a silliness that too, is empowering. And since it does have its lighter side, is a very much needed haven for repose. So what is this special word that is so likeable?

Eccentric

If you asked the people who have been around me for awhile what is the one thing I said I have always wanted to be when I grew up? They would tell you: "Susan wants to be *eccentric*".

Now all the times I have said this out loud, I have been talking about the silly side of eccentric, the unusual side of the family tree of this word. This is pretty much a human response. We all do it. We take a word, idea or phrase and use it in the context we know, the one we think we know. The one that will benefit us most, then we go with it. We go with it for as long as it suits our needs, then we let it go without fully knowing and embracing its entirety. This is a shame because we miss out on some good stuff! Let's take a closer look at the different sides of eccentric and find out why it's so important for you to be it, too.

The obvious is the one about your crazy aunt, who wears her underwear on the outside of her clothes, and everyone including you and Uncle Bob has labeled her, eccentric.

But I think eccentric has gotten a bad rap. Most people have taken Merriam-Webster's definition: *"Deviating from an established or usual pattern, or style,"* and twisted it into meaning deviant, as in abnormal instead of unusual. And what is wrong with unusual? Who wants to be usual all the time? Not me. I want to be eccentric in the way my dog Tillie exemplifies eccentric. She skips when she's happy. She also jumps and twirls at the same time. She is authentically a genuine original. She's truly one of a kind! That's what I want to be: a *"one of a kind"*.

And what is the key to being authentic?

Nurturing, I believe we must nurture ourselves. You must nurture yourself. You must cultivate what is *unique in you* and cherish what is *precious*. If you will do this you will become remarkable, remarkable to yourself and to others.

You must learn to value your individuality. If you don't how can you expect others to? Remember change always must start with you. Always, 100% of the time, change has to start with you. Others won't change unless they have to. You must be the reason and the catalyst for them to change. But don't change just in the hopes the other person will change. Because quite often they will disappoint you - you *will be* disappointed. They *won't* change the way you want them to, or they are *incapable* of changing. You will become resentful and think everything I have told you is just so much blah-blah-blah. That's because your *motive* was wrong. You can't change for others or change in order for others to change. You have to change for yourself, because you want it, you need it. And finally, you change because you realize change is the most important thing for you to do.

Motive, not an "E" word but it should be. Every action has a motive behind it. The things you do and say and what others do and say have motives behind them. You must continually be examining yours, to make sure your motives are pure – not calculating or manipulative. You must also *pay attention* and look for the motives of others. If their motives are pure then what they are saying and doing is coming from their authentic self. If they are being manipulative – STOP! Recognize it and don't become part of the manipulation.

So back to eccentric, release the elasticity (another fantastic "E" word) inside and stretch your flexibility muscles. This way you are ready to absorb the richness of your whimsical nature. That inner knowing that is unique to you, just like your fingerprint – one of a kind. Your whimsical will see the humor and the heart of any situation. It will enable you to identify innovative solutions that the logical part of you could never even dream of. Embrace this freshness, this originality, this "sparkle" inside. But don't just leave it there. It is meant to be shared with others. So break it out of jail, open the box, let it go, and let it run!

Let me share a funny story with you. My daughter sold her house and found a great one she wanted to buy. During the inspections a number of fairly serious issues popped up, making the house not so perfect. She had to decide whether to let go of this house and rent for a little while until she found the house of her dreams. Or go ahead and buy this house at a reduced price.

She was in a "tizzy" because she was feeling stressed, unsettled, and indecisive. She told me that logically it made sense to buy it. She could live in it for a while, build up some equity, sell it, and then look for the perfect one. But she didn't sound happy or excited. She felt like she was going against her gut, her inner knowing.

I told her, "You're right it does sound logical if you are a computer or robot." She started laughing and told me she felt like she was settling for an "arranged marriage". Now, I laughed at that one! I thought that was a great description of trying to make the best out of a bad situation. At the end of the conversation she asked me what I really thought she should do. I told her, "Well, it all depends whether you can live with your arranged marriage or not!" We both laughed some more and then she said she'd let me know her decision. I'm glad I didn't have to make that one!

What does that story have to do with our topic? Well, it is imperative that you are able to recognize your inner knowing. People used to call it intuition. There is a reason why your subconscious is trying to communicate with you. You must stay open to it. Stay tuned in to it at all times. This is something you nurture and must recognize is an important part of you. Once you are regularly in touch and communicating well with this part of you, then you will be able to use it to help guide you through difficult dilemmas. Don't underestimate that "gut" feeling – your intuition and "inner knowing" part of you which, just like your "picker" - can be broken and in need of repair. It may be almost non-existent due to your neglect. So *pay attention!* Pay attention to your inner knowing and your picker!

Again, you have a choice. You can either go with your gut or go against your gut. But the important thing is that you are informed. You are conscious of what your gut is telling you, sometimes screaming at you. You may pick the logical over your gut, or maybe your gut *will* turn out to be the logical thing. The important thing is that you are aware of your body, emotions, and feelings both consciously and subconsciously.

Work, work and more work... I know.

Now that we have talked about the lighter side of eccentric, let me tell you what I think may be the *really* interesting part of eccentric. An eccentric person is unforgettable. They leave their mark on your mind. They have made an impression and left a memory. That impression may be a good one or a not so good one, but it's there.

My husband is definitely eccentric. When people meet him they either love him or hate him, there is no gray area. We always hope for the "love 'em" bucket, but sometimes he's a drop in the other bucket.

Me? I am not quite that dramatic of a personality. Because of that I strive to be so purposeful and intentional with a sprinkle of whimsical that you are unable to forget me. I guess I'm just a natural-born cheerleader jumping about. It's important to me to leave my mark on you, and on the world. I want to make a difference in such a remarkable way that there is no doubt that I was here. I want to make sure I fulfilled my ultimate purpose. This means I want to be *brave enough to try, strong enough to persevere, sensitive enough to be on time, and humble enough to be a servant leader to those in my path.*

A short personal anecdote:

I love the color pink. Sometimes I have pink covering almost every part of me. I even have a hidden stash of purses, shoes, ink pens and stationary, etc... Often I decorate myself with as much of this stuff as I possibly can and go out shopping or running errands. Now, in itself, doing this might seem like the lighter side of the eccentric me - stretching my "whimsical" muscles. But that would be a mistake. Because you see, the bright colors and the fun trinkets are just my way to open up conversations and increase the opportunities to engage with others. Giving me the opportunity to leave my mark on them and helping me stay in line with my ultimate purpose. It actually is a calculated plan. It makes leaving a memory with them possible. Aha! In this way, I think everyone should want to be eccentric.

But it can't just be something chosen as a fleeting thought. If you choose to be eccentric you must embrace it fully and you must be it everyday. It must be so much what you stand for that others describe you that way. When they think of you - *eccentric* immediately pops into their head. Others will want to be around you because of it. Others will want to possess what you have and become what you are. Eccentric isn't something you own or buy or get as a gift. It's not something you win like the lottery. It *is* you. It is you without trying to be you or trying to be "it". It's your natural state of being. And because it is natural, it's the secret of why others want to be around you. You make them feel better. You make them feel better about themselves. You are illuminated and your light shines on the good, the positive, and on the possibilities in others. You are an illumination!

And right behind illumination you are a condiment. Huh? What? No joke you are like condiments. They are not a meal in themselves, but without them everything would taste bland. Life would be tasteless, unappetizing and boring. You spice things up. You compliment, "you little condiment you". So bring yourself to the picnic and practice your eccentricity until you are everything to be of it there is.

And since we are talking how without eccentric you may want to report off and call in sick for the day. Here is the next "E" word that compliments the "compliment". A word our true being wouldn't be complete without:

Essential

You may be wondering why I am bringing this up again because it feels familiar to you. As if we have talked about it before. In many ways we have since, all the "E" words we have discussed *are* essential to change and to your well being. Essential to your ability to discover and pursue your ultimate purpose, in this way, we are repeating ourselves.

Let's think of this as a little bit more, taking it a step further. Because it is more than we have talked about before, and different too! Now we are talking about the whole you, the *you* that *is* your total collective being. The *you,* that is everything you are and everything you represent. So now essential takes on a more expansive meaning and role in your life. It takes on some seriousness!

Let's talk examples. You are indispensible in your own life. So it is essential that you show up every minute of it every day. You are a required element. In fact, you are the *only* component, the only factor that is non-negotiable. *You are so essential to your life that if you don't show up, you are actually living someone else's life*! If you don't show up, you are not living the life you dreamed about. The life, that was designed solely and specifically for your ultimate purpose. If you don't intentionally show up in your life you will be living a life you weren't prepared for, a life you have assumed. And you know what happens when you assume; A–s-s-s-u-m-e and you make a ___ out of you and me. Well in this case, just out of you. It won't work out. It can't!

We have already discussed the importance of paying attention and being 100% mindful, all of the time. Stop, look, and listen. Like your mother told you to do before you crossed a busy street. But do it with everything and everyone every minute of every day of your life. That's how essential being present in your life is! That's how essential being fully present in; making decisions, in your relationships, in your career, and in taking care of yourself is. *It's the difference between, just living, and having "a life!"*

Remember you and I are "free-willers." That's how we were created. No one forces me to be me, or you to be you. No one forces you to sleepwalk through your life or to live life 100% engaged. *You choose.* And remember what happens when you don't? Not choosing *is still choosing*!

If you were a cake, you would be the flour. If you were a meatball, you would be the meat. And if you were a corn dog, you'd be both the corn and the dog. That is how important you are. You are the only ingredient that matters. Without you, there is no you. You will starve without you.

On the surface this may sound somewhat ridiculous. But I need you to seriously consider it for a minute. You have to start changing the way you think of yourself and what "you" and "being you" really means to support the change you want in your life. You can't just randomly think about it. You must act with authority, as the genuine unpolluted you. Live life as the bona-fide individual you were born. Act with the individuality into which you were born, the innocent, untarnished, uncorrupted, and incorruptible you. And please don't think I mean you are corrupt in that you have broken the law and should go to jail. Even though, it is a crime to lose your self. And for those who have done it, it feels like you are in jail, being held in a prison without bars.

Being uncorrupted, untarnished, and innocent means having the character with the strength and courage to be yourself. The innocence of character you had as a child. The one you had before you worried what people would think of you or how you looked in the mirror. Before someone told you people were different and should be treated differently. It's when you lived life full throttle, no holds barred and without worry. Worrying was left to the grown-ups.

This uncorrupted, untarnished, innocent and authentic person is what I believe all the great teachers and philosophers wrote about. What they tried to instill in us and teach us all to be. "Come as a child." I don't think all of this can be fully understood unless we come into it as a child; with an open mind, pure of heart and pure of soul. That is what I believe enlightenment is. What I believe being enlightened is all about.

So, am I crazy? I guess it is debatable depending who you ask. I hope the answer you get is an essential one and a little eccentric, too!

So what's the trick for being essential?

Don't believe everything you hear, see and you read. Think! Question! Pursue the answer! Pursue the truth! Smile, give people a break, give yourself a break, pay attention, don't settle, don't let anyone treat you less than, and don't you treat anyone else as if they were less than. Find the best in people, be an encourager, forgive, let go, create something that overwhelms your soul. Do something special for someone and feel your spirit soar. Look deep inside and acknowledge that *knowing* part of you who wants you to fulfill your dream, *your purpose.*

And don't let other people's misery become yours. Don't be a pessimist or a procrastinator. *Don't give up or give in*! Don't let others opinions define you. Don't let others define who you are! You are the only one who should define "you". Don't let one or 100 mistakes stop you. We all make mistakes. Don't think, "It's impossible" and don't say, "I can't".

How's that? And how's this?

"IF WISHES WERE..."

I have a movie in my head
I play it every night,
In the darkness of my lonely room
It's my sanity brought to light.
The pictures flip,
Reels and reruns never change.
You better not get near me
Because it may rub off on you.
In the darkness of your lonely room,
The "best of life," will be your reruns, too!

-Susan Farah

Don't let that be you!

Instead – let this be you - take a chance!

"DREAMS"
I want to float so high
That no one can reach me,
Not even you.
Drifting...for eternity.
Clouds for pillows,
Chantilly and tranquility.
No need for anything,
Just me... And clouds...

-Susan Farah

And our next "E" word is:

Entrust

Entrust is a powerful word. It is one of those words that sounds solid and feels impermeable. Nothing can penetrate it. It is a word that makes us feel safe, like someone has got our back. In our world of understanding and knowledge entrust oozes commitment, confidence and responsibility.

The truth is we have been entrusted. You have been entrusted. And since you've been entrusted - you must be trustworthy, worthy of trust. What have you been entrusted with? You have been entrusted with your purpose, the true reason for your being. As we've discussed, you have an ultimate purpose. One that is just for you. No one else can do it or should do it. It is yours alone. The sad part is that only some will find it and then live it. Many won't. They will leave themselves and others denied, wanting, and confused with life.

If you don't understand your purpose and allow yourself the opportunity to possess and live it, you will end up questioning life, asking your self, "Why am I here?" "What's it all about?" This leads to unfulfilled dreams, disillusionment, resentment and regret. And others will question your life too, confused as to who you are.

So let's talk more about this word, "en-trustworthy". I believe you understand being trustworthy. But, "en-trustworthy?" Why don't we start with taking the word apart and see if we can make sense of it. Let's start with entrust. From our Bing Dictionary, entrust literally means: *"To be given something with the belief that we will do what is expected."*

It is the gift of opportunity to help others. And this gift has been handed over and assigned to you by someone who has the confidence that you will not only do it, but do it commendably. Otherwise someone else would have been assigned to do it. Someone else would have been given the privilege. It would have been someone else's purpose.

Wow! And worthy, it implies that this commitment has been given with faith and trust in you. You are the most credible one and the most reliable one to accomplish it.

Entrusted is the expectation. Worthy is the belief. It is the belief that you will be steadfast and unfailing to the end. That you will continue to pursue your purpose no matter what, for as long as it takes. Even if that means it takes a lifetime. Even if you never reach what you believe is your ultimate goal. For you see, it is *the pursuit* that is your purpose – not necessarily reaching the goal.

Impressive isn't it? Or, is it scary and daunting? Is the glass half empty or half full? Don't be intimidated or overwhelmed! You don't have to be perfect or do it perfect, *you just have to do it and you will be perfect for the job!*

So how can you be a person of "entrust"?

You must accept. That's it. It's as simple as that, but just as complicated. Just accept that you have been entrusted with a purpose, an ultimate purpose designed only for you and that only *you* can accomplish. And out of obedience you have submitted (which is being obedient with respect) and accepted there is a bigger reason for you being here on this planet than just to buy a car that will rust, own a house that will get old, gather stuff that will collect dust, then die after this bag of bones and skin of yours gives out. Gee, I sure hope there's a better reason for you and me to be here than that! Don't you?

How are you on acceptance? It's crucial. So if you are one of those stubborn individuals and need to do some work on acceptance, get busy! You must accept that entrust is who you are and you will allow it, *"to be"*– you. You are entrust, entrust is *you*.

Our next eye-opener: "You are not alone." You are probably thinking, "No joke!" "Isn't that stating the obvious?" I mean all there needs to be is one other person and it makes sense, right? I wish it was that simple but the "alone" I am referring to has a whole other meaning.

No man is an island. You may have heard that one before too, but did your soul recognize it, or did it just bounce off you into outer space? It just doesn't mean that you can't do everything by yourself, or that you should ask for help if you need it. It means you are not just an individual You were not made that way. You were not created to live in a vacuum - isolated from others. You were wonderfully created to bond. It is your natural instinct to do so.

There's so much talk about animals and their natural instincts, but don't we realize we are no different? We have natural instincts too, innate to us humans. And since you are a human being we are talking about you! Bonding is probably the most deep-seeded one you possess. There have been many studies done as to what happens when babies miss out on that first "bonding" experience. How their lives have been altered and riddled with negative consequences without that personal touch, because it is paramount that the human spirit bond with another.

It is a hunger, a desperate need, which if goes unfulfilled will gnaw at your very soul. It is a rare human that lives their entire life as a recluse. Instead we live in tribes, colonies, villages and towns, cities small and large, rural and metropolitan. We form counties and alliances. We form teams and clubs, organizations and fraternal associations. We long for relationships, dating, marriage and co-habitation. All are solutions for belonging to and with someone else. Youths abandoned and left to their own devices will join gangs, even if the gang is violent in nature - just to belong to a group and not have to be alone. That is the nature of the beast. You are no exception.

Think of the movie, "Jerry McGuire" and the part when Jerry finally gets it. He hits that profound moment, that bonding brick wall. He realizes that it not only "wasn't all about the money," but that it "was all about sharing" the success or failure with his important someone.

There's a movie starring Kevin Costner, "For the Love of the Game" with a similar theme. Kevin's a baseball pitcher and pitches the perfect game, an incredible feat. But he ends up sitting alone in his hotel room, breaking down and crying, because the meaning of it all is lost without the one he needs to share it with. That's, the "perfect" human analogy.

Are you still having trouble grasping why entrust is so important? Let's do an experiment. Close your eyes and imagine you are back in time several hundred years. You are sitting under a tree on a sunny day minding your own business, when suddenly a very important-looking man rushes up to you, hands you a small silver box and says, "You must take this to the other side of the world and do exactly what the instructions inside say to do. And you must do it within the next five days or everyone on the planet will die!"

He goes on further to inform you that you are the only one who can do it. There is no one else who can. You are the one. *Without you, all is lost*!

What do you do?

Do you believe him? Or do you think to yourself that he's just some kind of nut? Do you wait around for the next five days worrying that everyone will die? Remember that includes you, too!

Or, do you see this as a challenge? Do you see it as your life's purpose, your divine purpose? Do you jump up immediately and start your journey with the hopes of completion and a bright future for everyone?

Now let's pretend this is a dead serious situation. You are a world-renown scientist and have just invented the cure for a deadly plague, which if not stopped within the next five days, will wipe out all human life. So you *are* the only one who can do it. There is no one else. You have been entrusted with this mission. It is your purpose for being born and being alive on this planet. Looks differently now, doesn't it?

We all have been entrusted. It could be you were created and entrusted to be the mother or father of the boy who became that scientist. It could be you were created to save, invent, encourage, nurture, stop, or start something that will change the world and save the lives of many. Or maybe you were entrusted to be an example, a helper, a giver, a soother and will give comfort and joy to many. Or maybe it's just one person. Who knows? And we may never know unless we take up the challenge, run to the end of the street, turn the corner and see what is waiting for us.

The truth is we are not here for ourselves alone. I know in

this day and age that goes against what many people think and believe. And it goes against what is being advertised and taught out there that: "I" is # 1 and morals and ethics are situational, irrelevant and old-fashioned. That there are different levels of the truth, and it is okay to "do whatever you have to do to get ahead," even if it means ruining someone else's life. Loyalty, patriotism and fidelity seem to be lost to a past when causes and principles were more important than one single person's comfort.

The truth is, *it's not all about us.* The truth is it's not all about you. It's all about your purpose. It is your legacy. It is that power inside you that drives you to be better, bigger, brighter and greater than you are. It is that invisible connection to your source, the greater good, your creator and architect who continues to lift you up and multiply your talents. It is that connection to your inspirer who inspires you to be more than you ever could be on your own.

Entrusted = en-trustable = **entrust.**

Does this describe you? Do you know what you have been entrusted with? Please take some time and think about this question. Put the book down if you have to. Think of this as a "crock pot" recipe. If you rush it you will be serving it undercooked.

Breathe...

Our next to the last "E" word is? Are we really almost done?

Have we traveled all this way and now are ready to close in on our destination? Have you thought about your progress in becoming the CEO of your life, recently? How are you doing? How is it coming along? What has gotten in your way? What have you learned about yourself? Have you changed, or did you say, "I'll do it tomorrow?"

"E" word number 26 is:

Efficacy

Thanks to Merriam-Webster we have our answer. Efficacy: *"The power to produce effects." "Energy of an agent or force."*

What stands out to you?

How about: *Driving Force – Power – Productive – Energy*

If you take a closer look you will see that together they intentionally bring something into being. In other words, efficacy is energy with the power to produce the effects that are wanted. *Self-efficacy* is energy (us - you), endowed with the power to bring into existence what was purposefully and mindfully intended to be created. More precisely, it is *"the belief that you have the ability and the capacity to accomplish anything and to deal with the challenges of life."*

How do you become rich with self-efficacy? How do you achieve it? Does everyone have it? Do some have more than others? What are the traits of a person who possesses it? And more importantly, "Is it the tangible power or is it the intangible belief that you have the power to do, to overcome, and to create the life you want?" And if it is just the belief, then why do individuals with similar skills and backgrounds seem to have mountains of it and the others are stuck in the valley with little or none?

This debate about the elusive efficacy and self-efficacy is fascinating but what is at the core of someone with it and someone without it?

Belief...the belief in yourself.

It is the belief that you are capable to do or to overcome. It's the belief that you have the "goods". That you have the intelligence, savvy, confidence, will, experience, strength and stamina to succeed. It's the "Whatever it takes" factor! Isn't that what this book is all about? Isn't it what you and I have been talking about and dissenting over the last days, and weeks?

When I talk about belief I just don't mean it flippantly. It isn't just, "Okay, I believe so it will happen" or "Now I can overcome it". Belief is a word of strength and made up of several layers giving it the stability it needs to withstand the hurricanes and tornadoes of life. You see, there is something underneath the belief. Something that is it's partner, it's other half. This other half, "the wind beneath its wings" has many definitions: ability, power, resilience, determination, resolve, buoyancy and optimism.

It is your grit. It is what makes you take a chance even though you may not know the answer, but you are willing to try anyway. It is the grit inside you that says, "I may not have that credential or experience but what I do have is comparable. And I will succeed!" It is the peace inside you that knows you can overcome whatever you are going through, because "this isn't the way it's supposed to end." And what do all these have in common? What does it all boil down to?

Purpose... It all boils down to purpose. It's about you knowing your ultimate purpose.

Everything you've experienced. Everything you've gone through. Everything you've learned, gives you the resiliency and self-efficacy to allow *efficacy* to be who you are – to be you.

When you know your purpose you can accomplish anything. You can literally overcome anything. You understand that you must and you will, *it's meant to be*. It is intended to be. Predestined and predetermined – *it's your purpose*. You have an ultimate purpose and it is *you*. To be 100% authentically you!

If it's alright I would like to give you one last exercise to do before you tackle our last "E" word.

Again I ask you to find a comfortable chair, relax and close your eyes. I want you to imagine you have a big black hole in your heart. This hopefully will not be hard to do since many people, including me, have felt like they really did have one at some point. Once you can see it, describe what that black hole does or how it makes you feel. What meaning does it have in your life? What emotions does it bring to the surface?

Next, I want you to picture yourself standing beside it with a shovel in your hand. What are you wearing? What does the shovel look like? Once the image of you and your shovel is real to you, I want you to see a large pile of dirt beside you. Feel yourself digging that shovel into the dirt, getting a big shovelful and sending that dirt flying down into that black hole. Watch yourself again and again piling shovelful after shovelful of dark dirt into that hole. Can you smell the richness and dampness of the earth? Keep doing this until the pile of dirt is gone and your hole is filled up. Pat the dirt down with your shovel until it is nice and level.

Look to your right and you will see a bag of grass seed. Open it up and sprinkle the seeds on the dirt. You will also see some straw lying there. Go ahead and spread some of it over the grass seed. Walk about twenty paces and you will see a water sprinkler, place it near your newly-planted seeds and turn it on. Watch as the droplets of water, like raindrops, gently soak your seeds, straw and dirt. You feel the warmth on your back and shoulders and realize the sun is shining down on you and the newly-planted grass seed. Take some time and feel the sun on your arms and face. Feels good, doesn't it?

Since there is no time – it has been suspended for you, the next thing you realize is that there are little green shoots of grass sprouting up all around you.

They are so green and fresh and new. What a good feeling to know you were a part of the miracle of their growth. You watch the grass grow taller and fuller and decide you want to do something more. You grab your shovel again and dig several small holes and begin to plant all sorts of flower seeds. As you are planting you are picturing in your mind what they will look like once they are in full bloom and bursting in all their glorious color.

More days of sunshine and gentle rain come along and before you know it buds of all shapes, sizes and colors are surrounding you. It looks like they are dancing to a merry tune as they sway in the wind. You take a deep breath. Oh! The smell is wonderful! You decide to add some trees or maybe some bushes to your garden. What about a trellis or white-picket fence? Maybe a rocking chair or bench to sit on as you rest and spend time in your garden.

You see some movement and hear some noises - butterflies and birds have decided to join you, sharing your tranquility. *Peaceful... Serene...*

Breathe....

When you are ready you can open your eyes. Remember you can make your experience as detailed and unique as you are. This exercise should last from ten to thirty minutes. It is what you make it. This is a powerful exercise. You may only notice a little feeling of peacefulness at first. *But you will be different!* A flicker of change has crossed your brain and something magical has danced across your heart. Expect something dramatic. Expect a miracle!

Essence

Essence is the culmination of all that has come before. It is everything we have been talking about. Essence, your essence, is what pulses through your veins. Essence is what surges along your brain's electrical pipeline. It is what speaks up, emanates, and shines out from you. But more than that, essence is your authentic self. It is your authenticity and no matter what has happened to you, what is happening now, or what may happen in the future it cannot be extinguished. It cannot be denied.

It is like the Olympic Flame. It burns brightest when lifted high and set free. Free to soak up oxygen and be that bright beacon of light blazing the trail. It can be stored but never lost. Always ready for the next opportunity to be lit and burn bright and true again. It's you in your full concentration, your concentrated self. It is your permanent element of being, your volatile quality that the substance which is *you* is made up of. It is your quintessence, your soul. Scholars have written books on this topic of essence, but it all comes down to this: If we can fix what's in our hearts, we can fix the essence of our being.

It doesn't matter if you are in a sad, depressing, or non-nurturing situation at this time. Your essence, your authentic light is not gone. It may be hidden. It may be burning dimly. It may feel as if it is in hibernation, but never fear - it is not gone. That is why no matter what the circumstances, there is always hope.

Don't give in to the fear, depression, or negative thoughts

that might tell you that you are not worth it. I don't think there is a soul alive who hasn't entertained these thoughts at some particular dark time in their life. I will be the first to admit that I have. I have thought of giving up and giving in. But if you can have just one thought of hope, one tiny speck, one mustard seed of a hope – just one; maybe things will change. This is enough to hang on to until it does, and it will. Change will come. It's the "hanging on" part that is crucial. You never know what could happen next and that is the spark, the "hope eternal" within all of us. We all have it. We were all born with it.

And as it is with your authenticity it can truly never be extinguished only lay dormant. But it is there, quietly waiting for you to allow it to have full reign in your life. Then that spark is a sparkle, and then a twinkle. It continues to multiply until it is a fully-breathing and heart-beating authentic life, your life – your essence.

Don't just take my word for it, read about it! There are so many stories of prisoners of war who have endured years of captivity, torture, and when freed had no hate in them. They had transcended the immediate and the physical. They had taken their essence to a place where it could survive and grow. Many stories of survivors of the Holocaust are beautiful examples in this same way. Not only did they not give up and turn bitter, they were able to use everything they had endured and allowed their architect to use it for the good of others.

I know it's hard to think that sometimes individuals

have to endure sickness, pain and terrors to fully fulfill their authentic purpose. But may I challenge your thinking for a minute? Question: "How do we know if something is good if we haven't experienced the bad to compare it too?" Open your mind and open the door for the goodness of: sickness vs healing = medical breakthrough, or disaster vs help = giving and philanthropy. Bad exists to bring out the good in people, only then good will emerge to replace the bad. Bad in this way has the job of releasing good, a tough job but someone has to do it. We don't always know the reason why this is true, but it's not our job to question. It's not debatable. "It's not our area". *It just is.*

As with everything, essence too, has its flip side. The "Bad Witch" essence... The one no one wants to be around. You know the tornado that wreaks havoc on anything and anyone in its path. The depressingly negative one that makes you feel like you can't breathe and makes your muscles cringe when you see it heading towards you. You can feel this one, too! It feels like that sticky, smelly dirt that you can't get rid of. The kind that makes you fly home as quickly as you can and jump into a scalding-hot shower.

I hope that one isn't you. Maybe it was you, but now, it's not you. We *can* be what we *want* to be. We can have what we believe. Because, "*We are* what *we believe* we are!"

It's our faith that defines us, faith in ourselves and in others. It's the ability to see the truth, which is the something *internal* and *eternal* that hopes to change the *external.* Read that one again. Let it really soak in.

It's the "who you were meant to be" embracing the "who you are trying to be" that ultimately will become the authentic you, the purpose-filled you.

Our essence is why we exist. It truly is our destiny, our purpose. It is the only true difference we can leave in this world. So trust your essence... Look around you. Inhale life's essence with every breath you take and exhale your essence into the life around you.

I hope you have found delight in all our travels together. It has been my pleasure.

May you have the wisdom to find your purpose and the courage to make a difference!

NOTES

Epilogue

Well, what do you think? Are you able to do it? Have you already started to change your life? Have you started on your road to a total life transformation? I hope so. Something I really believe is that all adults over the age of 30 or so are in recovery. We're all in recovery. It's called "Life Recovery". It's like the gate swung one way with all the things that have been done to us, all the things we have done to ourselves and all the things left undone. Then, the hinges on the gate got stuck and they wouldn't open any more. At that point we were left with two choices: to force that gate open doing the same things we have always done over and over again, which usually ends up with a broken gate. Or examine the gate with our architect who designed it, make the necessary changes so the gate works properly and swings open wide with ease.

And since I love eccentric sayings here's another one, "A parked car can't be steered too easily." So you better start your engine and get in gear, because you need to travel your "road of life" without going in the ditch.

I know now, my architect, put me here for a reason, a

purpose. And at age 59, I am sizzling with excitement to embrace it. I have envisioned my life the way it is supposed to be. And after close examination, I've chosen to accept that everything I have gone through and everything I have done has gotten me here. As a result, I have chosen the "Life Recovery" concept and am ready to travel this "road of life" transformed. Ready to utilize all that I have learned to reach my ultimate purpose, my reason for being here on earth.

How about you? What have you chosen?

Don't forget, "There is no fear, because fear is false evidence appearing real." Thank you, Dr. Dyer!

Instead try faith – F.A.I.T.H. – ***f****ully-***a****cceptable* ***i****nternal* ***t****hought-***h****ighway.*

-Susan Farah

Take a test drive down your faith and see how far you can go! See how far it takes you. You may be surprised at your destination.

So CEO, I can't wait to hear your stories and the fulfillment of your dreams. You better dream BIG because I love those "whale tales!"

Remember...

Trust + Faith + Forgiveness = Power. (TFF= P)

Oh, I do like that one! I think that's going to be the equation for one of my next books. Gotta dream big, right? TFF=P in action! I hope you have been inspired. I know I have been inspired traveling this journey with you, exploring and discovering.

So what is your "*Legacy*?" What have you done that no one else could do? What will you do that no one else will be able to? What will be whispered or shouted about you. Believed or misunderstood about you after you are gone?

I want to leave you with one last gift. We have made this journey together. Now you are a friend of mine, my new friend. So, as my new friend here is something my *best* friend taught me, *"You and I were born to shine."*

Our truest purpose is to let our light shine, bright and "eternal". So above all...

Believe...

Here's a freebie. I am leaving you with one last word. It's not part of the 27. It's "free". It is:

Everything

Everything = all things = all things are possible. So everything and anything is possible.

Change is possible.

You are living proof! Share it!

Illuminate!

Shine...

Trust...

P.S. **RUN YOUR RACE**!

Live life to its' fullest potential, don't back off, and please do the illogical.

What's the ending to your story? How do you know who others are unless you bring out the best in them? How do you know who you are unless the best is brought out in you? Look in the mirror, what do you see? It is you or is it only a reflection of you? Are you here by serendipity or by divine ultimate purpose?

Remember, don't let anyone tell you are less than. Your architect has just done a miracle through you. What is that miracle? The miracle is you, today and everyday!

And...

"Prepare for rain," don't pray for it. One you ask for and then wait. The other you act and live as if you have *already received,* there is no doubt. *You* have no doubt.

Your last exercise, write down in your *"Prepare for Rain"* journal: "I have two umbrellas - one in my house and one in my car, because it's raining (I am truly blessed) and I *know* it's going to be raining a lot more!"

In fact, I'm gonna get drenched!

Be Blessed!

Your friend,

Susan

ATTACHMENTS

Fill in the blanks to a "Changed You"

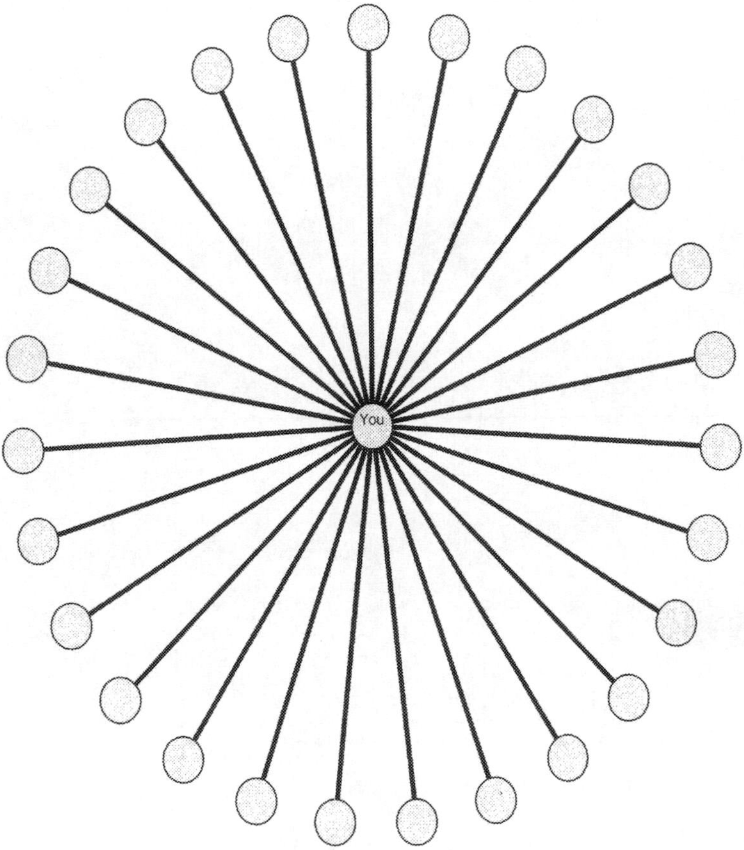

Fill in the blanks to a "Changed You"

THE 27 "E" WORDS THAT WILL CHANGE YOUR LIFE

Action Words

Embrace

Examine

Engage

Envision

Exhale

Excavate

Expand

Ecckk!

Endorphins

Encourage

Empower

Nouns – "To Be's or Not To Be's"

Equal

Excuses

Expectations

Emotions

Email

End-zone

Extraordinary

Endowed

Experience

Let It Be You, Adjectives – The Description of You

Energy

Evolve

Eccentric

Essential

Entrust

Efficacy

Essence

About the Author

Susan resides in Blowing Rock, North Carolina along with her husband, Tom, and their scrappy little dog, Tillie. Her book, *27 "E" Words That Will Change Your Life,* is her fourth in a series of inspired books and poems.